Ready-to-Use
REVISION &
PROOFREADING
Activities

UNIT 5

JACK UMSTATTER

Illustrations by Maureen Umstatter

**THE CENTER FOR APPLIED
RESEARCH IN EDUCATION**
West Nyack, New York 10994

Library of Congress Cataloging-in-Publication Data

Umstatter, Jack.
    Writing skills curriculum library / Umstatter, Jack.
        p.   cm.
    Contents: Unit 1. Ready-to-use word activities
    ISBN 0-87628-482-9
    1. English language—Composition and exercises—Study and teaching
(Secondary)—United States.   2 Education, Secondary—Activity
programs—United States.   I. Title.
    LB1631.U49 1999
    808'.042'0712—dc21   99-21556
                                                                                    CIP

Printed in the United States of America

10 9 8 7 6 5 4 3 2

ISBN 0-87628-486-1

**The Center for Applied Research
in Education**
West Nyack, NY 10994

http://www.phdirect.com

DEDICATED

To my grandmother, Louise Gavigan, for her love, spirit,
and willingness to accept life's changes and challenges.

ACKNOWLEDGMENTS

Thanks to my daughter Maureen for her artistic creativity and to my wife Chris for her many hours of work on this project. I couldn't have done it without you.

Thanks again to Connie Kallback and Win Huppuch for their support and encouragement with this series.

Appreciation and thanks to Diane Turso for her meticulous development and copyediting and to Mariann Hutlak, production editor, for her tireless attention throughout the project.

A special thanks to my students, past and present, who inspire these ideas and activities.

Thanks to Terry from WISCO COMPUTING of Wisconsin Rapids, Wisconsin 54495 for his programs.

Definitions for certain words are taken from *Webster's New World Dictionary, Third College Edition* (New York: Simon & Schuster, Inc., 1988).

ABOUT THE AUTHOR

Jack Umstatter has taught English on both the junior high and senior high school levels since 1972, and education and literature at Dowling College (Oakdale, New York) for the past nine years. He currently teaches English in the Cold Spring Harbor School District in New York.

Mr. Umstatter graduated from Manhattan College with a B.A. in English and completed his M.A. in English at S.U.N.Y.—Stony Brook. He earned his Educational Administration degree at Long Island University.

Mr. Umstatter has been selected Teacher of the Year several times and was elected to *Who's Who Among America's Teachers*. Most recently, he appeared in *Contemporary Authors*. Mr. Umstatter has taught all levels of secondary English classes including the Honors and Advanced Placement classes. As coach of the high school's Academic team, the Brainstormers, he led the team in capturing the Long Island and New York State championships when competing in the American Scholastic Competition Network National Tournament of Champions in Lake Forest, Illinois.

Mr. Umstatter's other publications include *Hooked on Literature!* (1994), *201 Ready-to-Use Word Games for the English Classroom* (1994), *Brain Games!* (1996), and *Hooked on English!* (1997), all published by The Center for Applied Research in Education.

ABOUT THE WRITING SKILLS CURRICULUM LIBRARY

According to William Faulkner, a writer needs three things—experience, observation, and imagination. As teachers, we know that our students certainly have these essentials. Adolescents love to express themselves in different ways. Writing is undoubtedly one of these modes of expression. We stand before potential novelists, poets, playwrights, columnists, essayists, and satirists (no comment!). How to tap these possibilities is our task.

The six-unit *Writing Skills Curriculum Library* was created to help your students learn the elements of effective writing and enjoy the experience at the same time. This series of progressive, reproducible activities will instruct your students in the various elements of the writing process as it fosters an appreciation for the writing craft. These stimulating and creative activities also serve as skill reinforcement tools. Additionally, since the lesson preparation has already been done, you will be able to concentrate on guiding your students instead of having to create, develop, and sequence writing exercises.

- Unit 1, *Ready-to-Use Word Activities*, concentrates on the importance of word selection and exactness in the writing process. William Somerset Maugham said, "Words have weight, sound, and appearance; it is only by considering these that you can write a sentence that is good to look at and good to listen to." Activities featuring connotations, denotations, prefixes, roots, suffixes, synonyms, antonyms, and expressions will assist your students in becoming more conscientious and selective "verbivores," as Richard Lederer would call them. Diction, syntax, and specificity are also emphasized here.

- The renowned essayist, philosopher, and poet, Ralph Waldo Emerson, commented on the necessity of writing effective sentences. He said, "For a few golden sentences we will turn over and actually read a volume of four or five hundred pages." Knowing the essentials of the cogent sentence is the focus of Unit 2, *Ready-to-Use Sentence Activities*. Here a thorough examination of subjects, predicates, complements, types of sentences, phrases, clauses, punctuation, capitalization, and agreement situations can be found. Problems including faulty subordination, wordiness, split infinitives, dangling modifiers, faulty transition, and ambiguity are also addressed within these activities.

- "Every man speaks and writes with the intent to be understood." Samuel Johnson obviously recognized the essence of an effective paragraph. Unit 3, *Ready-to-Use Paragraph Writing Activities*, leads the students through the steps of writing clear, convincing paragraphs. Starting with brainstorming techniques, these activities also emphasize the importance of developing effective thesis statements and topic sentences, selecting an appropriate paragraph form, organizing the paragraph, introducing the paragraph, utilizing relevant supporting ideas, and concluding the paragraph. Activities focusing on methods of developing a topic—description, exemplification, process, cause and effect, comparison-contrast, analogy, persuasion, and definition—are included.

- "General and abstract ideas are the source of the greatest errors of mankind." Jean-Jacques Rousseau's words befit Unit 4, *Ready-to-Use Prewriting & Organization Activities*, for here the emphasis is on gathering and using information intelligently. Activities include sources of information, categorization, topics and subtopics, summaries, outlines, details, thesis statements, term paper ideas, and formats.

- "Most people won't realize that writing is a craft." Katherine Anne Porter's words could be the fifth unit's title. Unit 5, *Ready-to-Use Revision & Proofreading Activities*, guides the students through the problem areas of writing. Troublesome areas such as verb tense, words often confused, superfluity, double negatives, and clarity issues are presented in interesting and innovative ways. Students will become better proofreaders as they learn to utilize the same methods used by professional writers.

- "Our appreciation of fine writing will always be in proportion to its real difficulty and its apparent ease." Charles Caleb Colton must have been listening in as Unit 6, *Ready-to-Use Portfolio Development Activities*, was developed. Students are exposed to many different types of practical writings including literary analyses, original stories and sketches, narratives, reviews, letters, journal entries, newspaper articles, character analyses, dialogue writing, college admission essays, and commercials. The goal is to make the difficult appear easy!

Whether you use these realistic classroom-tested activities for introduction, remediation, reinforcement, or enrichment, they will guide your students toward more effective writing. Many of the activities include riddles, hidden words and sayings, word-finds, and other devices that allow students to check their own answers. These activities will also help you to assess your students' progress.

So go ahead and make Mr. Faulkner proud by awakening the experience, observation, and imagination of your students. The benefits will be both theirs—and yours!

Jack Umstatter

ABOUT UNIT 5

Ready-to-Use Revision & Proofreading Activities, the fifth unit in the *Writing Skills Curriculum Library*, contains 90 creative, useful, and reproducible editorial activities that will help your students become more astute at editing their writings and enjoy themselves as they learn and/or review the editing skills. These activities can be used in many ways. Try them as an introduction, review, or remediation. Some can be a fifteen-minute filler, and others can function as a thirty-minute lesson. They are useful as quizzes, tests, homework assignments, or class competitions. Some of the activities use riddles, word-finds, and other fun devices that allow your students to check their own answers.

Section One, "Working Out With Words and Expressions," features eighteen activities dealing with plural words, abbreviations, possessives, words often confused, usage, definitions, clichés, idioms, and malapropisms. Three crossword puzzles are found here as well.

The next section, activities 19 through 35, "Making Sense With Sentences," includes seventeen activities that deal with writing sentences. Focusing on writing more mature, convincing sentences, students will edit fragments and run-ons, combine sentences more intelligently, and incorporate more details in their sentences.

"Grabbing Hold of the Grammar and Usage Problems," activities 36 through 55, offers twenty activities that take a comprehensive look at some of the more troublesome grammar and usage problems. Here students review the parts of speech, clauses, subject-verb agreement, irregular verbs, verb tense, dangling modifiers, correct pronoun use, and grammatical terms. A diagnostic usage test and a crossword puzzle are included in this section.

In Section Four, "The Editor's Desk," activities 56 through 75, students will improve their proofreading skills. Working as editors in most of these twenty fun activities, the children will review spelling, capital letters, apostrophes, commas, and double negatives. Additionally, they will work on identifying sentence components and writing more concise sentences.

The final fifteen activities found in " Moving On to Longer Writings" concentrate on revising longer types of writings. Starting with the sentence, moving on to the paragraph, and then working on the composition, students will understand what constitutes a powerful piece of writing. The business letter, the biographical essay, the dialogue, and other information-gathering activities are also found in this last section.

Your students will enjoy these ninety classroom-tested activities. Plus, since these reproducible activities are ready-to-use, you will be able to concentrate on the many other tasks you have as a teacher. So go ahead and watch your students' editorial skills improve. Their improvement will be your enjoyment!

Jack Umstatter

CONTENTS

SECTION ONE
WORKING OUT WITH WORDS AND EXPRESSIONS

SECTION TWO
MAKING SENSE WITH SENTENCES

SECTION THREE
GRABBING HOLD OF THE GRAMMAR AND USAGE PROBLEMS

SECTION FOUR
THE EDITOR'S DESK

SECTION FIVE
MOVING ON TO LONGER WRITINGS

TEACHER'S CORRECTION MARKS

ab	abbreviation problem	pr ref	pronoun reference problem
agr	agreement problem	pun	punctuation needed or missing
amb	ambiguous	reas	reasoning needs improvement
awk	awkward expression or construction	rep	unnecessary repetition
cap	capitalize	RO	run-on
case	error in case	shift	faulty tense shift
cp	comma problem	sp	incorrect spelling
cs	comma splice	thesis	improve the thesis
d	inappropriate diction	trans	improve the transition
det	details are needed	TX	topic sentence needed (or improved)
dm	dangling modifier	U	usage problem
dn	double negative	UW	unclear wording
frag	fragment	V	variety needed
ital	italics or underline	VAG	vague
lc	use lower case	VE	verb error
mm	misplaced modifier	VT	verb tense problem
num	numbers problem	w	wordy
^	insert	WC	better word choice
¶	new paragraph needed	WM	word missing
‖	faulty parallelism	WW	wrong word
,	insert comma		
pass	misuse of passive voice		

WORKING OUT WITH WORDS AND EXPRESSIONS

5-1. THE PLURAL PUZZLE

Thirty-two words in their singular form are listed as clues. For each word insert its plural form as the answer to that clue.

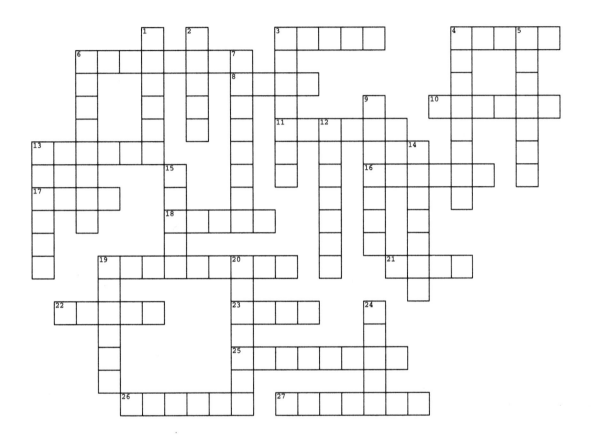

ACROSS

3. solo
4. tooth
6. church
8. ox
10. baby
11. video
13. rider
16. knife
17. deer
18. moose
19. country
21. foot
22. fly
23. datum
25. child
26. wolf
27. valley

DOWN

1. crisis
2. sheep
3. shelf
4. tomato
5. thief
6. comedy
7. soprano
9. monkey
12. dress
13. radio
14. fireman
15. woman
19. chief
20. index
24. goose

5-2. WORKING WITH PLURALS

Twenty-five plurals are listed below. On the appropriate line, write each word's singular form.

1. _____ roses

2. _____ videos

3. _____ oxen

4. _____ data

5. _____ fathers-in-law

6. _____ tomatoes

7. _____ media

8. _____ deer

9. _____ wishes

10. _____ mice

11. _____ lice

12. _____ waltzes

13. _____ pianos

14. _____ women

15. _____ wolves

16. _____ ladies

17. _____ children

18. _____ thieves

19. _____ roofs

20. _____ knives

21. _____ monkeys

22. _____ skies

23. _____ foxes

24. _____ leaves

25. _____ elves

5-3. THE ABBREVIATIONS PUZZLE

Twenty-nine abbreviations are listed as the clues. Write each abbreviation's full word or translation in the puzzle's appropriate spaces.

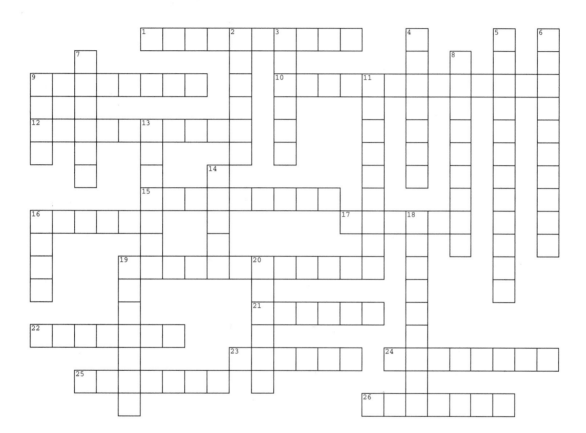

ACROSS

1. Lietu.	19. S.A.
9. Rev.	21. St.
10. M.D.	22. co.
12. A.D.	23. vs.
15. et al.	24. Mrs.
16. Jr.	25. Fla.
17. Sr.	26. hwy.

DOWN

2. i.e.	11. C.E.
3. no.	13. Ont.
4. Wm.	14. mo.
5. A.M.	16. Je.
6. e.g.	18. incl.
7. Ave.	19. Sen.
8. Blvd.	20. Mr.
9. Rd.	

5-4. WORKING WITH POSSESSIVES

On the appropriate line, write the possessive form of the expression adjacent to it.

1. _____ the bike belonging to June

2. _____ the mother of James

3. _____ the climate of Dallas

4. _____ the wages of laborers

5. _____ the story of Romeo and Juliet

6. _____ the speech of the union treasurer

7. _____ the opinion of everybody

8. _____ the stories of Poe and the stories of Twain

9. _____ the car belonging to the Jones family

10. _____ the attraction of the media

11. _____ the house they own

12. _____ the meowing of the cats

13. _____ the plans of the three companies

14. _____ the hat she owns

15. _____ the wallet belonging to my father-in-law

16. _____ the toys belonging to the children

17. _____ the increase of the taxes

18. _____ the activities of the sixth day

19. _____ the family of the author

20. _____ the eyeglasses belonging to Chris

© 1999 by The Center for Applied Research in Education

5-5. MRS. LIVINGSTON'S LIST

Mrs. Livingston, the English teacher, needs your help. She has just finished reading her students' essays, and she has compiled a list of words that her students commonly confused. In one instance, the student used **weather** when he should have used **whether**. That was a typical mistake.

Show Mrs. Livingston that you are a cut above her students. Below the word-find puzzle are the words the students mistakenly used. Locate and circle the words they *should* have used. They are written backward, forward, diagonally, and vertically. Then, on a separate piece of paper, define both words. There are 25 pairs of words. Be careful!

© 1999 by The Center for Applied Research in Education

```
D H G T Z Q T M J N J Q X R Y Y S J Q D Q D C Y
V T J X G Q J F P F P N Q N S W N J Z G W C H V
C F L V X R V Y B T V B V J D X P C C K B Y V B
T O C M Q H F B K L Q J V V S M P Q C R F V Z N
Y Z U H M S L Z C K A R N S A D V J L J B P D D
N D L N Z L H P X S B P F G S L J L O N D L C L
V D E M C D J H P X Q A I V S T O T T M D A B V
T K R R M I Y W N T F B R C E T H O H E M I R N
F O R M A L L Y R L E S S E N Y K T S H O N E R
L A A Y L F H F P B W D M E T I P E E E W H A T
K L T T M N R M W A G N M M X E R H E F T K K W
X L L S H C K Q S D S I Z Q C T B P N Q C F V X
S U A Q R R J Y L M L T V C Y T H Y Q C D M K J
F D C N T Z E V Z P M W A H R C H Z C L S A Z M
C E L B B H D W M V N H K S I W Z E Q M E W M D
Y Q V F H Q L O C F L Z J H T F G B R W V X N G
M D W N N C H J F S H W C Z M S T M E S F S F
```

alter	dessert	meat	than
ascent	elude	passed	their
bear	except	plane	through
brake	fair	principle	week
clothes	formerly	scene	witch
complement	lesson	shown	
counsel	lose		

5-6. WORKING YOUR WAY TO 45 WITH EVERY 2 OUT OF 5

Each sentence has one underlined word. Within each of the three groups, only two out of the five underlined words are used correctly. Add the numbers of the sentences in which the underlined word is used correctly and your total for all three groups should be 45. For the sentences in which the underlined word is used incorrectly, write the correct word after the sentence.

Group A

1. This is a <u>lesson</u> we will remember for a long time.

2. My coach <u>lay</u> the ball on the 34-yard line.

3. English classes enjoy debating the <u>morale</u> of this story.

4. Had Sheila known about the advanced sales, she might <u>have</u> purchased some tickets.

5. I advise you to contact the <u>personal</u> department of our company.

Group B

6. How many years have <u>past</u> since we last saw one another?

7. What is the scientific <u>principle</u> behind this phenomenon?

8. I like to meditate in this park because it is a <u>quite</u> place.

9. It is his <u>rite</u> as a citizen to say that.

10. Morty signed the letter, "<u>Respectfully</u> yours."

Group C

11. Can you believe what <u>they're</u> trying to do?

12. This is <u>too</u> much for him to take right now.

13. The custodian gave this room a <u>through</u> cleaning.

14. Do you know <u>wear</u> the children hid the cookies?

15. Please remain seated <u>wile</u> I look for your folders.

5-7. WHEN IS A BUILDING RAISED?
WHEN IS A BUILDING RAZED?

Thirty-two words that are commonly confused with other words are the clues in this crossword puzzle. For each answer, write the word that is defined in the clue. Thus, the answer to 2 Across is **brake,** a word commonly confused with **break.** Fill in the remaining 31 answers.

ACROSS

2. stopping device
6. without clothes
7. to be certain
10. past tense of lead
12. the ability to see
13. to build up
14. to avoid
15. the seat of government
18. an animal or to carry
20. a place
21. to level
22. forward
24. the building where the legislature meets
27. after third
28. a piece of wood

DOWN

1. not moving
2. smash
3. to abandon
4. forbearance
5. possessive of "you"
8. opposite of yes
9. to make letters
10. heavy metal
11. after-dinner course
15. to quote an authority
16. persons under medical care
17. something learned
19. ceremony
20. writing paper
23. not interested in
25. to refer to indirectly
26. opposite of increase

5-8. THREE IN A ROW

Write the letter C on the line next to any sentence that uses the underlined word correctly. Write the letter I next to any sentence that uses the underlined word incorrectly. If your answers are correct, you should see an interesting answer pattern.

1. _____ Before moving to Maine, the family had <u>formally</u> lived in Vermont.

2. _____ The young child rode on a float in the <u>Forth</u> of July parade.

3. _____ The traitor was <u>hung</u> for his misdeeds.

4. _____ An <u>eminent</u> psychologist had addressed our honor society.

5. _____ Since he did not seem to care about right and wrong, we could only describe him as <u>amoral</u>.

6. _____ What did you <u>infer</u> from her rather cryptic message?

7. _____ Hank was there in an <u>instance</u> notice.

8. _____ <u>Irregardless</u> of what they were thinking, they should not drink and drive.

9. _____ Our tour guide escorted us to the beautiful <u>Aisle</u> of Capri near Sorrento, Italy.

10. _____ We ordered some additional <u>lead</u> pencils for the conference.

11. _____ Fortunately, my middle school guidance counselor gave us good <u>advice</u>.

12. _____ Mrs. Phillips made several literary <u>allusions</u> during today's lecture.

13. _____ We noticed a large <u>amount</u> of mosquitoes near the lake this summer.

14. _____ There were <u>less</u> people here last year.

15. _____ We could not tell <u>witch</u> country he was describing.

5-9. WORDS WE OFTEN CONFUSE

The two choices in each sentence are words that are often confused. Circle the correct choice in each sentence and then write the word in the appropriate space next to the sentence's number. The number written after each sentence indicates which letter of the correct answer should be written at the bottom of this page. If your answers are correct, the letters spell out a major concern for any homeowner.

1. _____ Frank had to choose (among, between) the five photographs. **(2)**

2. _____ Jocelyn is a (good, well) player. **(3)**

3. _____ What did you (imply, infer) from his words to us? **(5)**

4. _____ Our social studies teacher has reviewed for the (passed, past) two weeks. **(4)**

5. _____ It was the most incredible (cite, sight) to see! **(3)**

6. _____ Ken tried to sew the (seam, seem) of his pants. **(3)**

7. _____ The athlete felt (altogether, all together) too tired to continue. **(5)**

8. _____ Jill held the (flair, flare) in her hands. **(5)**

9. _____ I don't have the (ability, capacity) to eat that much food. **(3)**

10. _____ The doctor detected a slight (brake, break) in the patient's arm. **(4)**

11. _____ It is very (liable, likely) that the concert will be rescheduled for next month. **(6)**

12. _____ The speaker intended to (imply, infer) exactly that! **(2)**

13. _____ Neither the (mail, male) nor female species is attracted to that plant. **(4)**

14. _____ They rolled the (cannon, canon) through the gymnasium and out the door. **(4)**

15. _____ Iron is a common (medal, metal, mettle). **(3)**

Write the specified letter of each correct answer in consecutive order on this line:

_____

What is a major concern for any homeowner? the _____

5-10. KNOWING THE DIFFERENCE

Selecting the best word for your description is important. Knowing the difference between the meanings of two similar words can make or break your reader's understanding of the described person, place, or thing. On the lines provided, explain the difference between the pair's two words.

1. pilfer/rob _____

_____

2. small/puny _____

_____

3. wash/scrub _____

_____

4. funny/hilarious _____

_____

5. house/mansion _____

_____

6. drink/guzzle _____

_____

7. frighten/terrify _____

_____

8. stumble/tumble _____

_____

9. save/hoard _____

_____

10. criticize/reprehend _____

_____

11. uncooperative/belligerent _____

_____

12. charm/captivate _____

_____

13. different/grotesque _____

_____

14. interest/mania _____

_____

15. jog/sprint _____

_____

© 1999 by The Center for Applied Research in Education

Name _____   Date _____   Period _____

5-11. IS IT THE RIGHT WORD?

Each group has only three sentences in which the underlined word is used correctly. If you total the numbers of the sentences in which the underlined word is used correctly, Group Two's total is double that of Group One. Circle the six correct sentences and correct the other fourteen in the spaces after the sentence.

Group One

1. He always likes to sit <u>besides</u> the baby.

2. The car's emergency <u>break</u> is now working properly again.

3. Mrs. Larsen has <u>born</u> two daughters.

4. The representative traveled <u>between</u> Frankfurt and Lisbon.

5. The basement pipe <u>busted</u> during the graduation party.

6. Our legislator had to <u>canvas</u> the area to ensure solid support in the election.

7. We should <u>have</u> asked for more food.

8. After the accident the family decided to hire a respected <u>council</u>.

9. Television is a very powerful <u>media</u> for disseminating information.

10. The 747's <u>descent</u> was monitored very carefully.

Group Two

11. Each swimmer <u>dove </u>into the pool to prepare for the race.

12. The <u>disinterested</u> judge was well respected for his fairness in all his trials.

13. Your version is hardly different<u> than</u> her version.

14. Quite frequently, parents and their children differ <u>with</u> each other on certain issues.

15. Their decision will have a major <u>affect</u> on what happens to that region.

16. Freshmen are usually <u>enthusiastic</u> about the upcoming school year.

17. I <u>insure</u> you that your ideas will be presented to the committee.

18. Everyone <u>accept</u> Marsha can help make signs for the fair.

19. The caring, generous older woman was <u>notorious</u> for helping the needy.

20. There are <u>less </u>items to be shipped today.

13

5-12. AVOIDING IDIOMS

Writers try to avoid idioms whenever possible. It is usually better to use fresher words rather than stale idioms. Each sentence contains an underlined idiom. In the space below the sentence, write a replacement for the idiom.

1. His incessant finger tapping was <u>driving me up the wall</u>.

   _____

2. He felt that he was <u>between a rock and a hard place</u>.

   _____

3. She felt she had <u>to grin and bear it</u>.

   _____

4. Roberta thought she was <u>in the catbird's seat</u>.

   _____

5. It was now <u>time to face the music</u>.

   _____

6. This was my chance <u>to kill two birds with one stone</u>.

   _____

7. It was a case of <u>the pot calling the kettle black</u>.

   _____

8. Early on in the contest, I knew that I was <u>in over my head</u>.

   _____

9. The families decided <u>to bury the hatchet</u>.

   _____

10. Steve had <u>put his foot in his mouth</u> too many times before that.

    _____

11. <u>Keep your ear to the ground</u>.

    _____

12. The detectives were <u>playing it close to the vest</u>.

    _____

5-13. CASTING AWAY THE CLICHÉ

Though this paragraph's writer has very positive things to say about her father, she has used an excessive number of clichés. *Tried and true* is the first of the many clichés she has included here. On the lines below, rewrite the paragraph eliminating the clichés. Share your new paragraph with your classmates.

My father is a tried and true good man. He is as gentle as a lamb. I can point out with pride that he seldom raises his voice. Dad is always cool, calm, and collected—something easier said than done! Additionally, my father, beyond the shadow of a doubt, has shouldered the burden of responsibility for his company. As wise as an owl, he had a sneaking suspicion that some company workers were taking items from the warehouse. Sober as a judge, Dad decided that he would find the leader of this covert operation. Though some said catching the kingpin would be like finding a needle in a haystack, Dad hit the nail on the head and caught the instigator. This evil man, now sadder but wiser, had to be brought back to reality and would have to face the music.

_____

_____

_____

_____

_____

_____

_____

_____

_____

_____

_____

_____

_____

_____

_____

_____

5-14. DON'T BE AS STUBBORN AS A MULE!

An English teacher has compiled a list of idioms that her students have used in their compositions this month. "As stubborn as a mule" was one such idiom. Idioms usually reduce a sentence's effectiveness.

Each of the 15 sentences includes an italicized idiom. Eliminate the idioms and improve the sentences. Write the new sentences on the lines provided. An example is done for you.

Example: He was *a wolf in sheep's clothing*. He was deceptive.

1. Camille's incessant nail biting was *driving me up a wall*. _____
    _____

2. Emil felt that he was *between a rock and a hard place*. _____
    _____

3. It was *like finding a needle in a haystack*. _____
    _____

4. Kim knew that she had *to grin and bear it*. _____
    _____

5. Unfortunately for the members, it was *time to face the music*. _____
    _____

6. Antonio and Charlie decided *to bury the hatchet*. _____
    _____

7. Keith believed our story *hook, line, and sinker*. _____
    _____

8. After only a few minutes into the contest, I knew I was *in over my head*. _____
    _____

9. This was Barney's chance *to kill two birds with one stone*. _____
    _____

10. It was certainly a case of *the pot calling the kettle black*. _____
    _____

11. Don't you think you are *cutting off your nose to spite your face?* _____
    _____

12. Agnes felt her promotion put her *in the catbird's seat*. _____
    _____

13. Stephanie had *placed her foot in her mouth* too many times. _____
    _____

14. The firefighters were *playing it close to the vest*. _____
    _____

15. It would be beneficial *to keep your ear to the ground*. _____
    _____

© 1999 by The Center for Applied Research in Education

5-15. WHAT EXACTLY IS ALL THIS?

Words are meant to communicate. When words are stuffy and beclouded, they confuse. The following paragraph is an example of unclear writing. William Lutz's book *Doublespeak* has many examples of doublespeak, words that make communication difficult for many different reasons. Words that Mr. Lutz includes in his book are underlined. Eliminate the underlined sections and replace them with clear, understandable words. Write your answers on the appropriate lines below the paragraph.

This summer I worked as a (1) petroleum transfer engineer. My work location was near fifteen acres of (2) underground condominiums. My building, equipped with (3) pupil stations, also had a (4) combustion enunciation unit. In my pupil station, I had an (5) emergency exit light, several honed (6) portable, lead, hand-held communication inscribers, a box of (7) interlocking slide fasteners for dental purposes, and (8) a manually-powered fastener-driving impact device. When they worked at night, all employees feared the possibility of an (9) involuntary conversion of property by one seeking financial assistance. One time a (10) certified adolescent transportation specialist needed to replace his yellow vehicle's (11) splash and spray suppression devices. My working partner and I performed the required steps necessary to perform this operation. My supervisor would accept no (12) inoperative statements from any company employee. If this occurred, the worker would become part of a (13) personnel downsizing.

1. _____

2. _____

3. _____

4. _____

5. _____

.6. _____

8. _____

9. _____

10. _____

11. _____

12. _____

13. _____

5-16. MAKING YOUR WRITING CLEARER

Writers use clichés and idioms sparingly since these overused expressions tend to make writing stale and predictable. The following paragraph includes many underlined idioms. Using the lines below (and the other side of this sheet, if necessary) rewrite the paragraph eliminating the idioms and including fresher, clearer words in their place. Feel free to use your dictionary.

My father is certainly a rags to riches story. Born into a poor family, he had his heart set on getting a good education. While attending law school, he would often burn the midnight oil. In two shakes of a lamb's tail, he was always willing to give the shirt off his back. He certainly was a hail fellow-well-met. Never would he pull the wool over someone's eyes and never would his actions raise eyebrows. In all situations he paid his dues as he took the bull by the horns. Even though law school forced many to keep their heads above water, Dad would always find a way to make hay while the sun was shining. Tough examinations did not give him cold feet. As luck would have it, he would usually study the material the professor selected as test questions. When he graduated from law school, Dad was at the top of his class. He was certainly the cream of the crop.

_____

_____

_____

_____

_____

_____

_____

_____

_____

_____

_____

_____

_____

5-17. MRS. LINKER'S CLASS

The students in Mrs. Linker's class have turned in their compositions. Most of the writings were very good; however, a few could use some improvement. One of the areas that caught Mrs. Linker's attention was the students' use of clichés and other overused expressions. Twenty examples Mrs. Linker spotted are included here. For each one, explain the expression's meaning by using more original and exact wording. Write your answers on the appropriate lines.

1. like two peas in a pod _____

2. cool as a cucumber _____

3. fat chance _____

4. smart as a whip _____

5. solid as a rock _____

6. once in a blue moon _____

7. raining cats and dogs _____

8. skinny as a rail _____

9. old as the hills _____

10. deader than a doornail _____

11. meek as a lamb _____

12. warm as toast _____

13. treat with kid gloves _____

14. listen in _____

15. sharp as a tack _____

16. stop on a dime _____

17. sly as a fox _____

18. give the shirt off one's back _____

19. make one's mark _____

20. leave no stone unturned _____

5-18. MRS. MALAPROP HAS TO GO!

Mrs. Malaprop, a character in Richard Brinsley Sheridan's play, *The Rivals*, has a knack for saying the wrong word. In the first sentence below, Mrs. Malaprop is confusing the words "hot plate" and the true part of the expression "hard place." Cross out the incorrect portion of each sentence and, on the line after the sentence, write the correct words. The first is done for you.

1. He was between a rock and a ~~hot plate.~~ hard place

2. We found out that he was a wolf in sheik's clothing. _____

3. I thank all of you for your comaraderieship. _____

4. Last year we studied about the Spanish Imposition. _____

5. You should be cognitive of what is ahead. _____

6. County residents were alerted about the salamander poisoning. _____

7. Our governor spoke about a beatification plan for our parks. _____

8. Mitchell's high school gradation ceremony was most interesting. _____

9. How much was the exercise tax on those foreign works of art? _____

10. The alfredo mural added much to the building's exterior. _____

11. Herman quenched his fists when he saw the enemy approaching. _____

12. Dr. Pike ordered a few anecdotes from the druggist. _____

13. Did you detect his subtle insinuendo? _____

14. Emily Post offers suggestions dealing with social adequate. _____

15. Rose recounted the hallowing experience in the dark alley. _____

16. The scientist found a cure for rabbis. _____

17. Since the members all wear the same type of clothes, this serves as an example of the group's infirmity. _____

18. Christine's reading pretention rate was average for a student her age.

    _____

19. Her arms were a limbo. _____

20. Werner purchased four quarts of milk at the local grievance store. _____

MAKING SENSE WITH SENTENCES

Name _____ Date _____ Period _____

5-19. SEVEN-UP

There are seven fragments, seven run-ons, and seven comma splices in these 21 groups of words. On the line next to the number, write F for a fragment, RO for a run-on, and CS for a comma splice.

1. _____ During a very difficult time in his life.

2. _____ The sun, appearing over the distant mountains.

3. _____ You will see the beauty of the mountains enjoy yourselves

4. _____ The couple walked along the shore, they were holding hands.

5. _____ Our country's civil rights story is memorable, many who lived through those times vividly remember the events.

6. _____ Noticing exactly what needed to be done for the ceremony.

7. _____ There are going to be some skilled writers in attendance we should go and listen.

8. _____ Find your way to the park by noon I will meet you for lunch.

9. _____ These crabs are delicious let us buy some for lunch.

10. _____ Never in a million years.

11. _____ All the time knowing quite well about it.

12. _____ Cave exploration can be exciting, more and more people are now spelunking.

13. _____ Can you understand this problem I think so.

14. _____ The financial crisis is the country's major problem, other countries are looking to see how it is solved

15. _____ Looking at the many options before us now.

16. _____ Last Sunday the church service was exceptionally memorable, many others felt the same way about it.

17. _____ Since you seem eager to take the trip.

18. _____ The royalty should be respected they are part of the country's history.

19. _____ The youngster closed the door on his hand, his aunt came to his aid.

20. _____ Another couple accompanied them to the wedding reception all of the people there enjoyed themselves.

21. _____ Golf is a game for patient people, it demands nothing less.

5-20. SENTENCE OR FRAGMENT?

If the group of words is a fragment, write *fragment* next to the number. If it is a sentence, write *sentence* next to the number. Then on the back of this sheet, write the corresponding letters of the fragments followed by the corresponding letters of the sentences. If your answers are correct, you will spell out a quote followed by the initials of the quote's originator. We will tell you his full name later.

1. _____ (LIF) The first activity in the book.

2. _____ (EIS) After he did the entire crossword puzzle.

3. _____ (YOU) Let's go.

4. _____ (ARE) We could see the fireworks from our kitchen.

5. _____ (MAK) The wave came right up to your chair, Greg.

6. _____ (ING) Explorers are a hardy group of people.

7. _____ (WHA) Whenever he feels the need to call his brother in Quebec.

8. _____ (THA) Fishing in the stream by his cabin.

9. _____ (OTH) Leafing through the magazine's pages, Danielle saw some interesting items.

10. _____ (ERP) Is this the best way to design the room?

11. _____ (PPE) During the hottest part of the summer.

12. _____ (NSW) To reach the summit of Mt. Washington with his team of climbers.

13. _____ (LAN) Because he could help his neighbor with the cleaning, he did.

14. _____ (HEN) Because they could not reach the canyon's bottom.

15. _____ (SJL) How did you do on this exercise?

© 1999 by The Center for Applied Research in Education

5-21. OLDIES BUT GOODIES

Here are some song titles from the past. Is each title a complete sentence or a fragment? On the appropriate line, write the letter F for the fragments and S for the sentences. Only eight of these titles are fragments. If necessary, ask Mom, Dad, Grandma, or Grandpa for help!

1. ____ "Could This Be Magic?"

2. ____ "To Sir With Love"

3. ____ "Since I Fell for You"

4. ____ "Daddy's Home"

5. ____ "It's My Party"

6. ____ "Please, Please Me"

7. ____ "You and Me Against the World"

8. ____ "Remember Then"

9. ____ "Have You Heard?"

10. ____ "I Wonder Why"

11. ____ "The Worst That Could Happen"

12. ____ "Don't Go Breaking My Heart"

13. ____ "Do You Love Me?"

14. ____ "Big Girls Don't Cry"

15. ____ "Help!"

16. ____ "I Think I Love You"

17. ____ "Starting Over"

18. ____ "To the Aisle"

19. ____ "Rock Around the Clock"

20. ____ "I Want to Hold Your Hand"

21. ____ "Love Me Tender"

22. ____ "You Belong to Me"

23. ____ "Hold Me, Thrill Me, Kiss Me"

24. ____ "Under the Boardwalk"

25. ____ "Bridge Over Troubled Water"

5-22. COMPLETING THE INCOMPLETE

Eight of the following groups of words are complete sentences and seven groups are either fragments or run-ons. On the line next to the appropriate numbers, mark the complete sentences with a C and the fragments and run-ons with an I. Each sentence has a two-letter code in parentheses after it. Write the two-letter codes of all the complete sentences on the indicated line at the bottom of this sheet. Then write the two-letter codes of all the fragments and run-ons (in order) on the appropriate line. If your answers are correct, the two-letter codes spell out a famous expression. The first part of the expression is found on the complete sentences line and the second part is found on the fragments and run-ons line. Thus, if you do all of this correctly, you have completed the incomplete!

1. _____ Please arrange the flowers while I am in the other room. (si)

2. _____ Unusual winds expected tomorrow. (do)

3. _____ Can you see if he will be there? (xo)

4. _____ Open doors are not allowed here in this secret place, shut that door immediately. (ze)

5. _____ Over the last two months of the football season. (no)

6. _____ It will probably never happen this way again. (fo)

7. _____ Because he was too old to play in the league, he signed up to be an umpire. (ne)

8. _____ Since he umpired so well. (fa)

9. _____ Casting his fishing line out to sea, the young fisherman. (no)

10. _____ During the final scenes of the movie, the people in front of us. (th)

11. _____ Twelve car dealers were called in to explain their advertising policies. (an)

12. _____ Rising to the occasion, the conductor persuaded the bully to leave the train. (da)

13. _____ Stop. (ha)

14. _____ Settling our differences more maturely. (er)

15. _____ Let us begin to settle our differences more maturely. (lf)

Complete sentences: _____

Fragments and run-ons: _____

The expression: _____

© 1999 by The Center for Applied Research in Education

5-23. FIVE ACROSS

There are five fragments, five run-ons, and five sentences in the following 15 groups of words. Write the term *Fragment*, *Run-on*, or *Sentence* on the appropriate lines.

1. _____ Even though they practiced for many hours each day.

2. _____ Let us start the match over, Martin.

3. _____ They passed them by, they arrived fifteen minutes late.

4. _____ Running along the tracks as quickly as possible.

5. _____ This is one of the most complicated problems.

6. _____ Seeing her family in the crowd of people, Samantha waved to them, they were happy for her.

7. _____ These stamps are valuable, you should store them in a very safe place.

8. _____ Whenever the opportunity presented itself to Tim.

9. _____ Flood waters ruined the downtown area, the townspeople are emotionally spent.

10. _____ There is a piece of gum stuck to the bottom of your seat.

11. _____ Nothing in the world.

12. _____ The best week of my life at Disney World.

13. _____ Brenda enjoys renting movies, she has rented over two hundred movies during the last two years.

14. _____ I am.

15. _____ Stop!

5-24. A COMPUTER GLITCH
(OR TWO OR THREE OR . . .)

This computer that Vicki bought has done nothing but give her trouble. For her English class homework, Vicki had to write eleven sentences and hand them in for a grade. Unfortunately, Vicki waited until this morning to print out the sentences—and was she in for a surprise! Though the words in every sentence were spelled and printed properly, the order of the words was incorrect. On the line below the computer's version of Vicki's sentences, write the corrected forms of the sentences. The word with the capital letter should be your sentence's first word. The first is done for you.

1. batter ball whacked the fast The.
   The batter whacked the fast ball.
   _____

2. under your your books Place desk.
   _____

3. way to is the get to best his This cabin.
   _____

4. that late is not open Our library.
   _____

5. school's best is the tennis She player.
   _____

6. our Two yard skunks were in.
   _____

7. a new purchased motor The family home.
   _____

8. program is on My favorite tonight.
   _____

9. He writing his just term paper finished economics.
   _____

10. arrive We for the comedian waited to.
    _____

11. The of serious need room is in cleaning.
    _____

5-25. OUT OF ORDER

Ten sentences are written below. Unfortunately, the words in each sentence are out of order. Rewrite each sentence as it logically should be written on the line below the jumbled sentence. The logical sentence's first word contains a capital letter. Compare your answers with those of your classmates.

1. go with He never group that will.

_____

2. fabulous Our is band.

_____

3. found was last disk The night.

_____

4. darkened strange objects filled is with room The.

_____

5. asking question you I am a.

_____

6. should all people treat You equally.

_____

7. parents to me want a be My mathematician.

_____

8. alley down the ball Gerald bowling the rolled.

_____

9. pretty sitting was He.

_____

10. you facts points make be must by the supported All.

_____

5-26. STRINGING THE WORDS TOGETHER

For each group of words, phrases, and clauses, construct a sentence. The words do not have to be placed in the order they currently appear. Write your sentences on the lines.

1. after . . . the skies . . . slowly

_____

2. wandering . . . police . . . briskly

_____

3. suddenly . . . two stores . . . emerged

_____

4. into the garage . . . automobile . . . dented . . . wall

_____

5. bracelet . . . beach . . . parking lot

_____

6. toenail . . . doctor . . . nurse . . . informal

_____

7. front . . . by . . . limousine . . . after the prom ended

_____

8. cushion . . . yesterday . . . poster . . . in . . . bedroom

_____

9. outlet . . . cord . . . garbage . . . street . . . morning

_____

10. after the flood subsided . . . weather . . . storm . . . relief

_____

11. stunned by the gun's report . . . elephant . . . circus . . . trainer

_____

12. serving dinner . . . mansion . . . skeptical . . . never

_____

13. next door . . . frequently . . . car . . . dog

_____

14. let . . . authorities . . . happened

_____

15. appointment . . . ferry . . . thirty . . . because

_____

Name _____ Date _____ Period _____

5-27. TEN OR FEWER

Complete each definition by adding fewer than eleven words to the words already given to you. Use your dictionary if necessary.

1. A circle is _____.

2. A comb is an object _____.

3. A couch is _____.

4. An umbrella is _____.

5. An ankle is _____.

6. A patent is _____.

7. A razor is _____.

8. A vagabond is _____.

9. An astronaut is _____.

10. A moccasin is _____.

11. A movie reel is _____.

12. A braid is _____.

13. A helicopter is _____.

14. A muscle is _____.

15. A lake is _____.

5-28. CONSTRUCTING SENTENCES BY THE NUMBERS

For each number, write a sentence containing that number of words. Thus, on the first line, the single word *Go* could be your sentence. Compare your sentences with those of your classmates. Enjoy!

1. _____

2. _____

3. _____

4. _____

5. _____

6. _____

7. _____

8. _____

9. _____

10. _____

11. _____

_____

12. _____

_____

13. _____

_____

14. _____

_____

15. _____

_____

5-29. LET'S EXPAND HERE

In some instances, short sentences are quite effective. At other times, the writer is better served by adding details such as adjectives, adverbs, prepositional phrases, and clauses. On the lines, rewrite each original sentence by adding more information to make the sentence more interesting. Share your sentences with your classmates.

1. We had a good time.

   _____

   _____

2. This was an interesting program.

   _____

   _____

3. Brett is a different kind of guy.

   _____

   _____

4. The waves at the beach were fine.

   _____

   _____

5. It was a nice experience.

   _____

   _____

6. She is a student.

   _____

   _____

7. Ralph made a unique comment.

   _____

   _____

8. That country could be better.

   _____

   _____

9. His books read easily.

   _____

   _____

10. The day was beautiful.

    _____

    _____

5-30. THEMATIC SENTENCES

For each group compose sentences that are related to the group's heading. Each sentence must begin with the letter that precedes the line. Thus, in the first group, WATER, the first sentence must begin with a word beginning with the letter W, the second with the letter A, and so forth. Try your best to have each sentence associated with the group's heading. Do not use the group's word itself in any of the sentences.

Group One: WATER

W_____

A_____

T_____

E_____

R_____

Group Two: MUSIC

M_____

U_____

S_____

I_____

C_____

Group Three: FAMILY

F_____

A_____

M_____

I_____

L_____

Y_____

Group Four: LIFE

L_____

I_____

F_____

E_____

© 1999 by The Center for Applied Research in Education

5-31. HELPING MR. HOPKINS

Mr. Hopkins, the school's new English teacher, has reviewed a set of papers that his students submitted. He wrote remarks next to some of his students' sentences and now he gives you the opportunity to see what he wrote on their papers—on one condition. Follow his suggestions (written within the parentheses) and make the changes he thinks will improve the sentences. Write your sentences on the lines provided and on the reverse side, if needed.

1. The weather was beautiful. We went swimming. (**Use a coordinating conjunction to combine these two sentences.**)

   _____

2. The mountain was breathtaking. We took a picture of it. (**Combine these two sentences using an adverbial clause.**)

   _____

3. Neil Armstrong was an American astronaut. He walked on the moon. He did this in 1969. (**Combine these three sentences using an adjectival clause.**)

   _____

4. Toni Morrison is a famous writer. She was raised in Ohio. She wrote the novel *Song of Solomon*. (**Combine these three sentences using an appositive.**)

   _____

5. Bob Dylan was a major force in the music world during the 1960s. Jim Morrison was too. (**Use a compound subject to join these two ideas.**)

   _____

6. Luanne walked past the living room. She glanced at the people in there. She did not speak to them. (**Combine these three sentences using an adverbial clause.**)

   _____

7. Brittany sprinted down the track. She heard the crowd cheer. She won the race. (**Use an adjectival clause to combine these three sentences.**)

   _____

8. The family went to church. Then they walked to the park. Later they ate dinner together. All this happened on Sunday. (**Combine these four sentences using parallel structure.**)

   _____

9. My sister had her baby yesterday. She and her husband are very happy. (**Combine these two sentences with the conjunction *since*.**)

   _____

10. Since the detectives were pleased with the remarks the witness told them, the detectives felt that they had some valuable leads in the case. (**Make this less wordy.**)

    _____

5-32. MATCHING THE SENTENCE'S TWO PARTS

Each sentence's missing portion is found in the list at the bottom of this page. Write the corresponding letter in the space within the sentence. Each missing portion is used only once.

1. His embarrassment _____ was obvious.

2. John's reluctance _____ was understandable.

3. Marnie showed her perseverance _____.

4. Louis was ecstatic _____.

5. Confusion reigned _____.

6. The supervisor chastised the workers _____.

7. Aaron's intellectual superiority was evidenced _____.

8. The athlete's strength was demonstrated _____.

9. Evelyn's agility was evident _____.

10. _____ Silas was quite the miser.

11. Ken showed his financial sagacity _____.

12. _____, Joe was a veritable prevaricator.

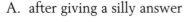

A. after giving a silly answer

B. after hearing he had been selected for the lead in the Broadway play

C. after seeing that they were far below their quotas for the month

D. as she maneuvered through the obstacle course

E. Because he seldom told the truth,

F. by checking over more than 14,000 applications that month

G. by his perfect scores on fifteen Advanced Placement examinations

H. by selecting seven profitable stocks

I. Hardly spending anything all the time,

J. to jump from the rock thirty-five feet above the water

K. when she lifted the heavy weight over her head

L. when the lead runner made a wrong turn

5-33. QUOTATIONS

The first half of these ten historical quotes has been separated from its second half. If you have a good sense of what constitutes a sentence, you will enjoy matching the two halves of each quotation. Write the correct letter of the quotation's second half next to its first half. The quotation's author follows the second half of the quotation.

1. _____ "Taxation without representation

2. _____ "I know not what course others may take,

3. _____ "Don't fire

4. _____ "We must all hang together,

5. _____ "To the memory of the men,

6. _____ "We have met the enemy and they are ours—

7. _____ "Go West, young man,

8. _____ "I will not accept if nominated

9. _____ "From Stettin on the Baltic to Trieste on the Adriatic,

10. _____ "We're eyeball to eyeball

A. Two ships, two brigs, one schooner and one sloop." (*Oliver Hazard Perry*)

B. first in war, first in peace, first in the hearts of his countrymen." (*Henry Lee*)

C. an iron curtain has descended across the continent." (*Winston Churchill*)

D. and grow up with the country." (*Horace Greeley*)

E. is tyranny." (*Patrick Henry*)

F. or assuredly, we shall all hang separately." (*John Hancock*)

G. and will not serve if elected." (*William T. Sherman*)

H. until you see the whites of their eyes." (*William Prescott*)

I. but as for me, give me liberty or give me death." (*Patrick Henry*)

J. and (I think) the other fellow just blinked. (*Dean Rusk*)

5-34. CRAZY QUOTATIONS

Ten quotations have been badly mixed up. The first half of one quotation has been mistakenly joined with the second half of another. Fix these quotes by writing the correct quote in the appropriate line below the mixed-up quotes. The quote's author precedes the first half of the quote.

1. (*Knute Rockne*) "Winning isn't everything, you won't be called on to repeat it."

   _____
   _____

2. (*John Dewey*) "The aim of education should be to teach children to think, that help themselves."

   _____
   _____

3. (*Harry Truman*) "The only thing new in the world and absolute power corrupts absolutely."

   _____

4. (*Benjamin Franklin*) "God helps them not what to think."

   _____
   _____

5. (*Lord Acton*) "Power tends to corrupt, who serves the country best."

   _____

6. (*Rutherford B. Hayes*) "He serves his party best are condemned to repeat it."

   _____
   _____

7. (*Jean Jacques Rousseau*) "Man is born free, is the history you don't know."

   _____
   _____

8. (*George Santayana*) "Those who cannot remember the past is the contamination of air, earth, rivers, and sea . . . "

   _____

9. (*Rachel Carson*) "The most alarming of all man's assaults upon the environment it's the only thing."

   _____

10. (*Calvin Coolidge*) "If you don't say anything, and everywhere he is in chains."

   _____
   _____

© 1999 by The Center for Applied Research in Education

5-35. THE BIG CONCERT

The four sentences below have been combined in ten different ways. Circle the number of each sentence that has correctly combined these four ideas.

> A. We bought concert tickets.
> B. The concert is in July.
> C. We waited on line for six hours to get the tickets.
> D. Each ticket was thirty dollars.

1. The July concert tickets, thirty dollars each, purchased after a six-hour wait.

2. For thirty dollars each and a six-hour wait, the concert in July tickets were bought.

3. In July, the concert tickets, purchased after a six-hour wait on line, were thirty dollars.

4. We waited on line for six hours and paid thirty dollars each for the July concert tickets.

5. For the concert in July we waited on line for six hours and paid thirty dollars for tickets.

6. For a six-hour wait and thirty dollars, we bought tickets to July's concert.

7. We bought July's thirty-dollar concert tickets after we waited on line for six hours.

8. Thirty-dollar tickets for a July concert were bought after six hours waiting.

9. After waiting on the line for six hours, we purchased thirty-dollar tickets for the July concert.

10. July concert tickets were purchased after a six-hour wait for thirty dollars.

GRABBING HOLD OF THE GRAMMAR AND USAGE PROBLEMS

5-36. INDEFINITE PRONOUNS AND WATER

If the indefinite pronoun in the sentence agrees in number with the verb, circle the letter preceding the sentence. Using those letters only, the letters will spell out, in order, two types of bodies of water. Write their names at the bottom of the page.

1. **(L)** Several of the boys on our team is traveling on the tournament by train.

2. **(I)** One of these girls swims two miles each day.

3. **(O)** All these people expects an easy day at work tomorrow.

4. **(S)** Most of the newspaper is wet.

5. **(N)** Some of the breads is not for sale.

6. **(T)** Everyone on these six lists does his or her best.

7. **(H)** Both of these automobiles are equipped with many extras.

8. **(G)** Somebody call our house every other day to sell us some tickets.

9. **(M)** One of these rockets was used as the museum's model.

10. **(U)** Another of these animals eats much food.

11. **(E)** Nobody in these classes have been selected for the scholarship.

12. **(S)** Either the umpire leaves or I leave.

13. **(S)** Nothing I do for these adults goes unnoticed.

14. **(T)** None of my friends was there.

15. **(O)** Both the cheerleaders and the bus driver wants to stop for some food.

16. **(R)** Neither of these products meets my standards.

17. **(A)** Something on the grocery counter is leaking.

18. **(I)** Everybody loves somebody at least once.

19. **(T)** Many of the baseball cards are priced quite fairly.

20. **(L)** Each of the cells need to be examined before we leave.

The two bodies of water are _____ and _____.

5-37. BE THE TEACHER

Here are the answers that John Q. Public wrote for his Parts of Speech Test. He was directed to write the part of speech of each sentence's underlined word. See how well he did by examining his answers and then, if necessary, correcting those incorrect responses by writing the correct answer in the space following the sentence. Each answer is worth five points. How well did John Q. Public do? Circle the number of any wrong answers. Then write Mr. Public's score on the line below the last question.

1. adjective _____ The funny man made the audience laugh hysterically.

2. noun _____ Each car had its own number.

3. conjunction _____ I wanted to see that movie, but I had to go out with my family instead.

4. pronoun _____ This violin was given to Tom and me as a present.

5. verb _____ Can you make this problem go away soon?

6. interjection _____ "Hey! That was my seat," said the young boy.

7. adverb _____ They walked through the darkened halls quite cautiously.

8. preposition _____ After the examination, the students went to get some food.

9. noun _____ We will very often see that family in town.

10. conjunction _____ I want to see him again for I know he is moving in a few weeks.

11. adverb _____ Never again will he be that excited.

12. pronoun _____ The group members decorated the floats by themselves.

13. adjective _____ Though she also likes September, my aunt's favorite month is June.

14. preposition _____ We enjoyed the play entitled *Into the Woods*.

15. adverb _____ As Molly parked her car, she remarked, "This is a tight squeeze."

16. noun _____ Leslie is the hostess at our local restaurant.

17. verb _____ Is this going to be our last chance to see you, Terry?

18. conjunction _____ "Our dessert will be delivered shortly," said Francine.

19. pronoun _____ Will you be traveling across the country for the next few months?

20. adjective _____ It is the most effective and the most inexpensive way to buy a car.

John Q. Public's score is _____%.

Name _____   Date _____   Period _____

5-38. FINDING A MATCH

Nine 7-word sentences are in Group A. Their mates, listing only the parts of speech, are in Group B. Match these sentences by writing the letter from Group B in the appropriate space in Group A. If your answers are correct, the consecutive letters will spell out two words associated with an infant. Write those two words on the lines at the bottom of this page.

Group A

1. _____   He walked slowly with the precious vase.

2. _____   In the morning we will have practice.

3. _____   You should ask him for his autograph.

4. _____   I am tall, but he is taller.

5. _____   The sacred text was found near Rita.

6. _____   They were removing the tree limbs carefully.

7. _____   You and she will perform quite soon.

8. _____   May the road rise to meet you.

9. _____   Send the package with the correct materials.

Group B

A. Pronoun—helping verb—main verb—pronoun—preposition—pronoun/adjective—noun.

C. Pronoun—verb—adverb—preposition—article—adjective—noun.

D. Pronoun—verb—adjective—conjunction—pronoun—verb—adjective.

E. Pronoun—helping verb—main verb—article—adjective—noun—adverb.

L. Article—adjective—noun—helping verb—main verb—preposition—noun.

O. Helping verb—article—noun—main verb—preposition—verb—pronoun.

R. Preposition—article—noun—pronoun—helping verb—main verb—noun.

T. Pronoun—conjunction—pronoun—helping verb—main verb—adverb—adverb.

Y. Verb—article—noun—preposition—article—adjective—noun.

The two words associated with an infant are _____ and _____.

45

5-39. PARTS-OF-SPEECH FILL-INS

Write the part of speech above the 16 underlined words in these sentences. Then, using the numbers corresponding to the eight parts of speech, write that number in the space after each sentence. If your answers are correct, each group's total will add up to the same number. Write that number within the parentheses after the group's name.

Noun = 1	Verb = 3	Adverb = 5	Preposition = 7
Pronoun = 2	Adjective = 4	Conjunction = 6	Interjection = 8

Group One (___)

1. <u>Neither</u> of the doors needed to be repaired. ____

2. There are ways that we could easily employ <u>to</u> do the job properly. ____

3. The comic had everyone laughing <u>heartily</u>. ____

4. How many <u>rotations</u> did the object make within an hour? ____

Group Two (___)

1. Can you <u>remember</u> the final question on the driver's exam? ____

2. It was only a short while before the dentist walked <u>into</u> the office. ____

3. Your family is a <u>wonderful</u> group of people. ____

4. The library will not be open for the next two days due to the <u>snow</u>. ____

Group Three (___)

1. We would love to attend, <u>but</u> we have other commitments. ____

2. Slowly but <u>surely</u>, the problems seem to be going away. ____

3. They could probably go by <u>themselves</u>. ____

4. Are you saying that our <u>bicycles</u> are not allowed on the train? ____

5. <u>Students</u> who play on school sports teams usually do well academically. ____

Group Four (___)

1. <u>Hooray</u>! We will be going to the state finals. ____

2. Are they rehearsing past twelve o'clock <u>again</u>? ____

3. <u>Each</u> of the fortune cookies we opened brought a chorus of laughter. ____

5-40. CLAUSES

Clauses are essential to good writing. Using effective clauses can improve your writing and make your sentences more mature and interesting. Fill in the blanks with your own words to complete the independent and dependent clauses. Share your answers with your classmates.

1. Although _____, they would never
   _____.

2. If _____, you will always
   _____.

3. Marty _____ because
   _____.

4. Since _____, the meteorologist
   _____.

5. While _____, Richard and his cousin
   _____.

6. In order that my choir _____, we must
   _____.

7. The _____ unless my motorcycle
   _____.

8. _____ even though the lake
   _____.

9. I _____ why the weather
   _____.

10. He _____ as if
    _____.

11. These girls _____ rather than
    _____.

12. They wanted _____ how you
    _____.

5-41. DO YOU AGREE?

Each sentence contains a problem in which the subject does not agree in number with the verb. Change the verb to make the subject and verb agree. Write the correct verb form on the line after the sentence's number.

1. _____ "Your version of the requirements are wrong," Ben told Jerry.

2. _____ "My idea of how faith, hope, and charity can be shown in our daily lives are easy to understand," Laurel told Hardy.

3. _____ "The captain, as well as the members of his outstanding crew, were at the banquet," Mutt told Jeff.

4. _____ "Measles are a major concern," Dr. Pepper told Dr. Dolittle.

5. _____ "Near the storage bin is my old suitcases," Moe told Larry and Curly.

6. _____ "There is a few players currently signing autographs," Tinkers told Evers and Chance.

7. _____ "Either of you are capable of the job," Ricky told Lucy and Ethel.

8. _____ "Some of the roads is not passable because of the storm," McNally told Fodor.

9. _____ "Some of the condiments is expensive," Heinz told Gulden.

10. _____ "Many of the contestants has been interviewed," Alex told Vanna and Pat.

11. _____ "Either the soldier or his comrades is to be questioned," George told Ike.

12. _____ "I are one of the greatest players of all time," Air Jordan told Magic.

13. _____ "Both the musicians and the audience member is ready to go," McCartney told Jagger.

14. _____ "Every one of the clowns, animals, and other performers are ready," Barnum told Bailey.

15. _____ "Six divided by three equal two," Euclid told Pascal.

5-42. DETECTING THE WRONG VERBS

Only four of these 20 sentences contain verbs that are used correctly. If the underlined verb is used incorrectly, write its correct form in the space next to the question's number. If the underlined verb is used correctly, make no marks next to the sentence. For each sentence in which the verb is used incorrectly, write the sentence's 3-letter code on the line at the bottom of this page. After you have done that for the 16 incorrect sentences, you will have spelled out, in order, four names. The activity's title will then make sense.

1. _____ **(MIS)** I had not <u>saw</u> him before the incident occurred.

2. _____ **(SMA)** The police <u>seeked</u> our help in the investigation.

3. _____ **(BRI)** He had not <u>meant</u> what he said to you.

4. _____ **(RPL)** Many of the phones had <u>rang</u> already.

5. _____ **(EHE)** Suddenly it <u>begun</u> to rain.

6. _____ **(RCU)** The second baseman <u>thrown</u> the ball back to the pitcher.

7. _____ **(LEP)** A few of the animals have nearly <u>froze</u> to death.

8. _____ **(OIR)** After the game we <u>shaked</u> hands with the winning team.

9. _____ **(SOR)** The girls and boys had <u>swum</u> in the lake last year.

10. _____ **(OTS)** An angry man had <u>swunged</u> his bat at the intruders.

11. _____ **(HER)** Have you <u>brung</u> your cooler to the beach?

12. _____ **(LOC)** Yesterday the sun <u>rised</u> at 6:31.

13. _____ **(KHO)** Some of the recruits had <u>ran</u> after the suspect.

14. _____ **(BCO)** Several pages were <u>torn</u> from the textbook.

15. _____ **(LME)** The ground <u>shaked</u> violently due to the earthquake.

16. _____ **(SFA)** The children had never <u>rode</u> horses before.

17. _____ **(ARN)** We <u>drove</u> two hundred miles to get here!

18. _____ **(THE)** Two of our basement pipes <u>bursted</u> last winter.

19. _____ **(RBR)** The precious gems had been <u>stole</u> from the bank's vault.

20. _____ **(OWN)** Two lifeguards have <u>went</u> out to save the man.

3-letter codes: _____

The four names are: _____

They are: _____

5-43. HAS HE ATE THE WHOLE PIE?

Your English teacher would cringe if you asked this. The correct form, of course, is "Has he *eaten* the whole pie?" Each of these 15 sentences contains an incorrect verb tense form. On the lines following each sentence, write the correct verb form. Make sure you cross out the incorrect form.

1. Yesterday I eaten vary sparingly. _____

2. Have you ever swimmed in the Pacific Ocean? _____

3. That teen has growed three inches this year. _____

4. The waitress shaked the bottle's contents on the food. _____

5. Three portraits were hanged in the local museum last week. _____

6. When the runner slided into second base, she hurt her ankle. _____

7. After he shot Abraham Lincoln, John Wilkes Booth fleed the scene. _____

8. While playing in the park, the small child was stinged by the bee. _____

9. Once the sun rised, we were more awake. _____

10. Thomas has always dreamt of acting on the Broadway stage. _____

11. Nobody in our family had rode in the Central Park carriage before yesterday.

    _____

12. Soldiers had raisen these flags over the fort. _____

13. Unruly spectators had throwed objects toward the playing field. _____

14. Ten minutes after finishing his dinner, Seth laid down for a brief nap.

    _____

15. I have wrote down all the steps we will need to follow. _____

5-44. USING THE CORRECT VERB TENSE

Using the correct verb tense is a must for the good writer. The verbs in eight of these 15 sentences are used correctly. Seven other sentences contain verbs that use improper verb tenses. Circle the letters of the eight sentences that utilize verbs correctly. Then unscramble the eight letters to form the names of two types of bodies of water. Write those answers at the bottom of this page.

A. After the game concluded, we celebrated at the manager's house.

B. Since we knew Steve's locker combination, we arrange to pull a practical joke on him.

C. If you can help me, I will have had appreciated it.

D. Whether you choose to leave or stay, I will go along with your decision.

E. They walked along the darkened trail and saw someone coming from the other direction.

H. The window close on the guitarist's fingers.

I. Dorothy had picked up the phone, but she had hear no one on the other end.

J. Because he had answered your question, you had respond back to him.

K. Wherever I travel, I see many people much like myself.

L. Daria should have done the job, but she chose not to.

M. In case Sheila comes by, told her I went to the supermarket.

N. Each of us can complete the projects, but more time will be needed.

O. The offer made by the management was quickly rejected by the union members.

P. If I help her collect the money, I can earn more pay.

Q. Look at the bruise I get last night in the rugby match.

Eight letters: _____

Two types of bodies of water: _____ and _____.

© 1999 by The Center for Applied Research in Education

5-45. IRREGULAR VERBS

The present forms of 35 verbs are the clues in this crossword puzzle. Using the present form clue, write the irregular verb's past participle as the answer. Thus, for 2 across, since the clue is *break*, the correct answer is the past participle of the word *break*, namely *broken*. Now think of the answers for the other 34 irregular verbs. Be careful!

ACROSS

2. break	19. sing
5. lose	20. leave
6. stand	22. slide
9. write	25. lend
11. sleep	26. arise
14. say	27. hold
15. cut	
16. spring	
17. keep	
18. become	

DOWN

1. let	14. shake
2. bring	15. come
3. know	16. steal
4. do	18. burst
6. swim	19. speak
7. rode	21. freeze
8. flee	23. draw
10. throw	24. pay
12. find	25. lead
13. choose	

5-46. DOING THE EIGHTY-ONE

A while back, a singing group named Candy and the Kisses had a hit song entitled "Do the Eighty-One." This activity is in honor of that song since the number of those sentences in which the underlined word is used incorrectly adds up to 81. There are five sentences in which the underlined word is used correctly and ten in which it is used incorrectly. On the line after the question's number, write **C** if the word is used correctly and **I** if it is used incorrectly. If the word is used incorrectly, write the correct word on the line following the sentence.

1. _____ Those people could have done the work by <u>theirselves</u>. _____

2. _____ All of <u>youse</u> can be there by eleven o'clock? _____

3. _____ The winner of this month's contest is <u>she</u>. _____

4. _____ A special award has been given to <u>them</u>. _____

5. _____ Packages had been delivered to both Dale and <u>him</u>. _____

6. _____ <u>Us</u> customers should not tolerate such poor business practices. _____

7. _____ Our two newly elected officials, Walter and <u>her</u>, can settle this immediately.

   _____

8. _____ Will you be able to do all this work by <u>yourselfs</u>? _____

9. _____ Several of the ferocious waves were a challenge to <u>we</u> swimmers. _____

10. _____ Our school's flag seems to have lost <u>it's</u> newness. _____

11. _____ Leslie and <u>her</u> are buying the tickets for entire group. _____

12. _____ My cousins had a difficult time finding <u>they're</u> way to the family reunion.

    _____

13. _____ It was <u>I</u> who gave you the cryptic message. _____

14. _____ Perhaps we can ask <u>her</u> now. _____

15. _____ <u>Him</u>, who was there during the spirited meeting, can tell us exactly what

    occurred. _____

© 1999 by The Center for Applied Research in Education

5.-47. DRIVING TO WORK LAST FRIDAY, DAD WAS IN BLOOM

What? Did I read this title correctly? Dad was in bloom? What does *that* mean? Actually, what the writer wanted to say was, "The flowers were in bloom while dad was driving to work last Friday." Now that is something quite different from the original sentence which contains a dangling modifier. This phrase "dangles" because it does not logically refer to another word in the sentence.

Eight of the following sentences contain dangling modifiers that should be placed correctly. Write the corrected sentences on the lines. You may add or delete words in order to make the sentence read correctly. On the other hand, if the original sentence is correct, leave it as it is. To check your work, the total of the numbers of the correctly written sentences adds up to 34.

1. Skiing down the hillside, the other mountain looked huge to Roger.

_____

2. After washing the dishes, the doorbell rang.

_____

3. Running after the intruders, the gun was shot by the homeowner.

_____

4. Walking along the city street, the tourist admired the sights.

_____

5. Weary from the strenuous workout, the weights were placed back in the closet by Hank.

_____

6. When electing a new president, the ballot should be filled in properly by the voters.

_____

7. Before leaving for her freshman year at college, Maureen was visited by her relatives.

_____

8. Thrown by the first grader, the teacher picked up the rubber ball.

_____

9. While doing homework, Laurie's cat scratched Laurie.

_____

10. To understand the intricate workings of the machine, the parts must be studied by you.

_____

11. While a member of Congress, Charles Smith, a Rhode Island representative, often rode a horse.

_____

12. Before delivering the good news, the newscaster coughed.

_____

5-48. LUCKY THIRTEEN GRAMMAR MATCHING

Match each of the 13 grammatical terms in Group One with its underlined example in Group Two. Write the two-letter answer in the space next to the appropriate number. A mountaineer was asked once why he wanted to climb Mt. Everest. If your answers are correct, you have spelled out both the response to that question and the name of the mountaineer who said it. (**Hint:** The author's first name is abbreviated.) Write the answer letters in order on the line at the bottom of this page.

Group One

1. _____ adjective clause

2. _____ adverbial clause

3. _____ comma splice

4. _____ declarative sentence

5. _____ exclamatory sentence

6. _____ fragment

7. _____ gerund phrase

8. _____ imperative sentence

9. _____ infinitive phrase

10. _____ interrogative sentence

11. _____ participial phrase

12. _____ prepositional phrase

13. _____ run-on

Group Two

AL. <u>Winning by a large margin,</u> the next governor thanked his workers.

BE. The cat <u>that you bought</u> is cute.

CA. <u>Since the weather is so beautiful,</u> let's go to the beach.

EI. <u>Here is the money, Irene.</u>

GE. The participants wanted <u>to play a few more games</u>.

HE. <u>Sliding down the hill on a tray</u> was fun for the college students.

LO. Perry walked <u>by himself</u>.

OM. <u>Are you going to the store now?</u>

RE. <u>Do it now, Josephine.</u>

RY. <u>I am going to the movies I want you to go along.</u>

ST. <u>In the middle of the thrilling performance.</u>

TI. <u>I want it all!</u>

US. <u>This is the best way to do it, the results will bear me out.</u>

Write the answer letters in order: _____

5-49. DIAGNOSTIC TEST OF USAGE

Each sentence contains an error in usage. In the space provided, write the correct form of usage. Each correct answer is worth five points. After your teacher goes over the answers, write your score in the appropriate space. Good luck!

1. _____ There is a huge number of togetherness in this fraternity.

2. _____ All of the contestants danced good last night.

3. _____ Kerry has less friends than you have.

4. _____ We all know that Diana should of chosen the other dog.

5. _____ She is a dancer which can move so gracefully.

6. _____ I can't get no satisfaction.

7. _____ The boys solved the problems theirselves.

8. _____ Please divide the candy between the five girls.

9. _____ Every golfer accept Hank Lyons plans to go to the charity tournament.

10. _____ Being that my grades were not good, my parents made me study longer and harder.

11. _____ Laura ain't going to listen to my sister's advice.

12. _____ Though we looked everywheres, we could not find the lost puppy.

13. _____ The kindergarten class can't hardly wait for the holiday vacation.

14. _____ Leave me do this part of the project by myself.

15. _____ The police officer walked in the garage and saw the hidden fireworks.

16. _____ Her uncle he will become a doctor next year.

17. _____ The clerk treated the customer very respectively.

18. _____ Gino is faster then the others in his team.

19. _____ Did you consider how this would effect your good name?

20. _____ The magician showed us many optical allusions.

Score = Number of correct questions (____) × 5 = _____ %

5-50. ONE TO A SENTENCE

Each sentence below contains one error in grammar or usage. There are no misspellings. Cross out the error and on the line after the sentence, write the correct form.

1. The pilot could of landed the plane earlier.

   _____

2. There are less smokers today.

   _____

3. They hadn't ought have done that to the clerk.

   _____

4. She don't need our help now.

   _____

5. Irregardless of what you say, the others want to go to that park.

   _____

6. Its just that you could not have done much better.

   _____

7. Who else, beside Traci, will be attending that college?

   _____

8. Shaneeka Collins is the most favorite of Mrs. Leward's students.

   _____

9. Television is his favorite media.

   _____

10. The diver jumped off of the highest diving board.

    _____

11. Their are many new members in the organization.

    _____

12. Eddie is a most unique runner.

    _____

13. She is the lady which is responsible for the program's success.

    _____

14. Does anyone know where the food is at?

    _____

15. Orange juice is a very healthier drink.

    _____

5-51. PROBLEMS...PROBLEMS...PROBLEMS

Each of these twelve sentences contains a different writing problem. On the line next to each number in Group One, write the corresponding letter from Group Two that exemplifies that problem. Each item in Group Two is used only once.

Group One

1. _____ Each of the trees were decorated beautifully.

2. _____ Where do you want to go on saturday?

3. _____ The present was given to Todd and she.

4. _____ The weekly magazine was published once a week.

5. _____ The car stalled, it could not be restarted that afternoon.

6. _____ A news bulletin was released it said a disaster had been averted.

7. _____ Seeing an opportunity for advancement, the job was taken by the woman.

8. _____ The family has a subscription to The New York Times.

9. _____ Mrs. Louise Gavigan was born on April 17 1900.

10. _____ The newspaper was read by his wife.

11. _____ The English professor phoned the dean, and he talked to him for ten minutes.

12. _____ As soon as the program began, the boy knock on my door.

Group Two

A. capital letter

B. comma missing

C. comma splice

D. misplaced modifier

E. passive voice

F. pronoun case

G. redundancy

H. run-on

I. subject–verb agreement

J. unclear pronoun

K. underline title

L. verb tense

5-52. DO YOU KNOW YOUR GRAMMAR AND USAGE?

Match each underlined portion with its description from the list below. Write the correct letter on the space next to the number. The first one is done for you. Each answer is used only once.

A. adjective

B. adverb

C. appositive

D. comma splice

E. faulty parallelism

F. fragment

G. idiom

H. incorrect adjective form

I. incorrect punctuation

J. incorrect verb tense

K. misplaced modifier

L. participial phrase

M. past tense verb

N. predicate adjective

O. predicate noun

P. relative pronoun

Q. run-on

R. subject

S. subordinating conjunction

T. transitional word

U. wrong pronoun

1. __B__ Our vacation is <u>always</u> exciting.

2. _____ <u>Reading the odometer</u>, the mechanic was surprised by the car's condition.

3. _____ Several <u>units</u> of blood were rushed to the accident scene in Washington, DC.

4. _____ The coin, <u>a 1973 penny</u>, was examined by the numismatist.

5. _____ Sly is the best <u>performer</u> on the tour this summer.

6. _____ Everyone will agree that Loretta is <u>friendly</u>.

7. _____ The <u>stringent</u> rules the organization imposed stifled the workers' creativity.

8. _____ He likes green beans; <u>however</u>, he doesn't like corn.

9. _____ They <u>studied</u> abroad for several semesters.

10. _____ This is the watch <u>that</u> I misplaced.

11. _____ <u>Written in beautiful printing</u>, the calligrapher presented the certificate to the recipient.

12. _____ Are you leaving for home so soon<u>.</u>

13. _____ <u>Although</u> the work is difficult, college is a great learning experience.

14. _____ Yesterday the campers <u>swum</u> at the amusement park.

15. _____ The band members have written music, recorded songs, and <u>likes to tour</u>.

16. _____ <u>Even if all the boxes of candy are sold before the end of September.</u>

17. _____ <u>Please carry this piece of luggage with you it's too heavy for me.</u>

18. _____ He is <u>off the wall</u> today.

19. _____ <u>Our van is durable, it has over one hundred thousand miles on it.</u>

20. _____ Mr. Thomas is the candidate <u>who</u> we have selected for the job.

21. _____ This is the <u>most perfect</u> setting for their honeymoon.

5-53. ASSESSING SOME SKILLS

Match each item in Group B with its description in Group A. Write the corresponding letter on the line next to the number. If your answers are correct, the consecutive letters will spell out a city, a baby's name, and hairy items. Write those three words on the line at the bottom of this page.

Group A

A. plural forms of words that end with "-um"

B. examples of imperative sentences

C. words commonly confused

E. words used as nouns and verbs

G. subordinate clauses

I. collective nouns

L. pronouns that could be indirect objects

M. plural words considered as singular

N. double negatives

O. plural nouns commonly misused as singular

R. passive voice verbs

S. transitional expressions

T. correlative conjunctions

U. clichés

W. titles that should be underlined or italicized

Group B

1. _____ statistics—news—athletics

2. _____ wages—pants—scissors

3. _____ don't never—hadn't none—can't not

4. _____ either/or—neither/nor—both/and

5. _____ were distributed—was brought—is brought

6. _____ trick—panic—stick

7. _____ bacteria—data—media

8. _____ me–them—him

9. _____ capital/capitol—complement/compliment—loose/lose

10. _____ as dead as a doornail—as thick as thieves—as cool as a cucumber

11. _____ Do as I do.—Hit the road, Jack.—Bring it here.

12. _____ Macbeth—To Kill a Mockingbird—Fahrenheit 451

13. _____ jury—flock—troop

14. _____ as soon as he is done—whenever they are curious—since the bell has rung

15. _____ for instance—on the other hand—otherwise

© 1999 by The Center for Applied Research in Education

Words are: _____

5-54. NATIONALITIES ARE IN—TRUE OR FALSE?

Write the word *True* or *False* next to each statement. Then write that number's corresponding two letters in the appropriate space at the bottom of this page. If your answers are correct, the consecutive *True* answers will spell out two nationalities, and the consecutive *False* answers will spell out two other nationalities.

1. **(CA)** _____ An adjective can modify another adjective.

2. **(AM)** _____ A gerund is a verbal.

3. **(NA)** _____ "Me" is a nominative case pronoun.

4. **(DI)** _____ The word "tooth" does not have a spelling change to form its plural.

5. **(ER)** _____ Titles of magazines should be underlined or italicized.

6. **(AN)** _____ The word *mechanize* can probably act as more than one part of speech.

7. **(AU)** _____ If a sentence contains a direct object, it must also contain an indirect object.

8. **(ST)** _____ If two words are joined by the conjunction "and," they must always take a plural verb.

9. **(IC)** _____ A clause must have at least a subject and a verb.

10. **(RI)** _____ Contractions are quite acceptable in formal writing.

11. **(AN)** _____ A sentence's subject that ends with the letter "s" can take a singular verb.

12. **(JA)** _____ "Who," "which," and "that" take verbs that agree with their antecedents.

13. **(PA)** _____ The pronoun "you" can be either singular or plural.

14. **(NE)** _____ A complex sentence has one independent clause and at least one subordinate clause.

15. **(SE)** _____ A compound sentence has two or more independent clauses and no subordinate clauses.

16. **(AN)** _____ An infinitive must include the word "to," the base form of the verb, and an adverb.

TRUE _____

FALSE _____

Name _____ Date _____ Period _____

5-55. TEN...TWENTY-SIX...SIXTY-FIVE

Within each group, circle the number of each sentence in which a pronoun is used incorrectly. Then total the number of those sentences. If your answers are correct, the total for Group One is 10, Group Two is 26, and Group Three is 65. Finally, correct each pronoun mistake in the space after the sentence.

Group One

1. This is the man whom you can ask.

2. Lilly and me are going to the same college in a few years.

3. Only us freshmen are allowed to attend the meeting.

4. Both they and I will help you to research your topic.

5. The winners are Kristine and her.

Group Two

6. The club's officials looked forward to his agreeing.

7. Whom told you that?

8. Our new principal is a godsend for us.

9. Please tell whoever you like.

10. Michael did it completely by hisself.

Group Three

11. Both candidates, him and her, look forward to the debate.

12. The soda was drunk by him and she.

13. It is me.

14. Miguel is the one whom selected this restaurant.

15. The presentation was judged by Ms. Stevens and I.

THE EDITOR'S DESK

5-56. THE INFAMOUS TWENTY-FIVE

Each sentence contains one misspelled word. In each instance, cross out the incorrect spelling and write the correct spelling on the line next to the question's number. Then write the first letter of the correctly spelled word on the line at the bottom of this page. If your answers are correct, the 25 letters you have written on that line will spell out, in order, three words associated with writing. Good luck!

1. _____ My friends and I love to play minature golf.
2. _____ The bride was allmost late to her wedding because of the traffic congestion.
3. _____ Is it necesary that we all get there at the same time?
4. _____ Does he always act so unusualy childish in front of adults?
5. _____ You must learn to supress your anger when things are not going your way.
6. _____ My sister loves choclate ice cream the best.
7. _____ He needed to ask his former boss for a referance.
8. _____ Most likely, the outcome was inevitabel.
9. _____ The sign warned that motorists should procede with caution through that intersection.
10. _____ Did you hear what today's temperture is, Kyle?
11. _____ This is the begining of a tough time in her life.
12. _____ Let this serve as a rememberance of our time together.
13. _____ Can you believe how much knowledge he has aquired in such a short time?
14. _____ I understand that her mother is a very influenshial person in this town.
15. _____ The family still owes the restaurant ninty dollars.
16. _____ Males and females live in seperate quarters in that college's dorms.
17. _____ Which of your teamates is the most skilled soccer player, Ozzie?
18. _____ We welcome you to this most solemn occassion.
19. _____ Whom would you reccomend for the firm's new position?
20. _____ Have you thought about applying for a second morgage on your existing home?
21. _____ He was described as one of the most elagible bachelors in the small town.
22. _____ How do you think she will do in her sophmore year?
23. _____ George sacraficed many things to become that successful.
24. _____ Jose agravated his injury by running too hard during practice.
25. _____ Several smaller boats accompanied the yahct on its way into the harbor.

The 25 letters: _____

Three words associated with writing: _____

5-57. SPELLING SOLUTIONS

All 30 words found below this crossword puzzle are misspelled. For each corresponding clue number, write the *correct* spelling of that particular word. Good luck!

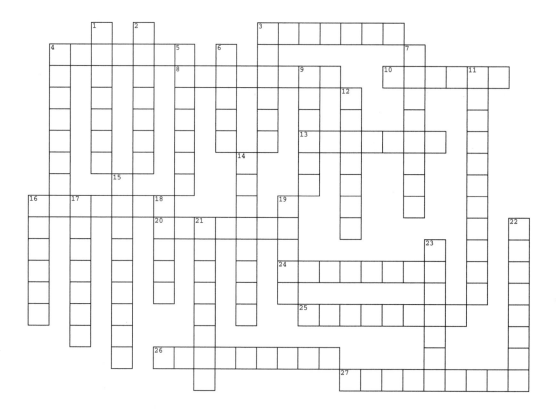

ACROSS

3. villian
4. initiel
8. exercize
10. patato
13. trafick
16. reciept
20. recieve
24. remembber
25. acurate
26. surprized
27. reconize

DOWN

1. biskit
2. finelly
3. vacum
4. imobile
5. liesure
6. meddal
7. hospitel
9. suttle
11. transfered
12. trajedy
14. midicine

15. dissappear
16. realy
17. collonel
18. truely
19. wierd
21. cemetary
22. praktice
23. writting

5-58. COMPLETING THE SPELLING

The 15 words below are waiting to be put back into their proper places. They have been taken out from the 15 sets of letters below the box. In Column A, write the word that makes the word in Column B complete. Then write the complete word in Column C. If your answers are correct, each word is used only once. The first word is done for you.

able	ice	member	oar	rig
ant	liar	meter	ort	rovers
dance	mar	noun	recede	them

Column A	*Column B*	*Column C*
1. ___liar___	auxiy	___auxiliary___
2. _____	ance	_____
3. _____	gram	_____
4. _____	domin	_____
5. _____	irate	_____
6. _____	re	_____
7. _____	unpnted	_____
8. _____	prefer	_____
9. _____	hse	_____
10. _____	conty	_____
11. _____	cey	_____
12. _____	atten	_____
13. _____	mgage	_____
14. _____	notable	_____
15. _____	maatics	_____

5-59. SPELLING SUCCESS

Each trio of words has one misspelled word. Circle that word's letter and write the letter on the line at the bottom of the page. Do the same for all the trios. If your answers are correct, you will spell out a sentence concerning spelling in today's technological world. Lastly, spell each misspelled word correctly next to the word itself.

1. (R) category
    (S) amatuer
    (T) forty

2. (P) twelvth
    (Q) definite
    (T) ninety

3. (C) playwright
    (D) absence
    (E) articel

4. (J) opinion
    (K) perform
    (L) persue

5. (K) rhythm
    (L) sacrafice
    (M) permissible

6. (C) relevent
    (D) height
    (E) parallel

7. (F) doesn't
    (G) excellent
    (H) truely

8. (D) fulfill
    (E) rember
    (F) across

9. (B) analyze
    (C) anallysis
    (D) repetition

10. (I) braggart
    (J) meant
    (K) breif

11. (C) pseudonym
    (D) chocolate
    (E) vannilla

12. (R) personaly
    (S) vacuum
    (T) nucleus

13. (S) apreciate
    (T) procedure
    (U) ninth

14. (Z) schedule
    (S) managment
    (B) psychology

15. (Q) erroneous
    (R) calender
    (S) existence

16. (E) seperate
    (F) desperate
    (G) calculate

17. (M) different
    (N) herroic
    (O) guarantee

18. (O) cupfulls
    (P) radius
    (Q) discipline

19. (S) symbol
    (T) dilema
    (U) cemetery

20. (P) foriegn
    (Q) forfeit
    (T) quantity

21. (E) lisense
    (F) villain
    (G) syllable

22. (Q) choir
    (R) chimnies
    (S) privilege

23. (R) superior
    (G) patroll
    (G) distinct

24. (D) antique
    (E) wanderful
    (F) flowery

25. (B) bashful
    (C) similiar
    (D) humble

26. (T) temperture
    (U) consonant
    (V) resemble

Answers spell out: _____

5-60. CAPITAL LETTERS

The sentences below contain 38 examples of incorrect capitalization. They either *should* or *should not* be capitalized. Circle the first letter of each word that fits this description and write those letters on the line at the bottom of this page. If you have correctly identified the 38 mistakes, you will have spelled out a quotation. Write that quotation on the line at the bottom of the page.

1. wyatt earp was a famous Lawman.

2. Our church group traveled to europe and africa during the past few years.

3. Mr. Harrington assigned Mark Twain's *The Adventures of Tom Sawyer* to be Read by november 15.

4. Some famous french chefs visited the conference.

5. The republican Party held a fund raiser in orlando last May.

6. They sent a congratulatory note to miss eccleston, the xerox representative.

7. Robert Frost won the Pulitzer prize.

8. Several Early Reformers played a large part in india's history.

9. Shakespeare wrote during the reign of elizabeth I.

10. We mailed the rebate to a company called northern canada express transit.

11. We attended the autograph session held by the Baltimore orioles and the New York Mets.

12. Your Doctor's Office will open at Ten o'clock this Tuesday morning.

13. My dad and I studied in halifax, a city directly East of here.

14. The band members decided to go, Regardless of the situation.

15. The indigo girls entertained the customers at harvey's tavern, a music hall in tampa, Florida.

16. He was described as "Hilarious and Interesting."

17. My cousin's Niece, Roberta Rosen, married a Guy who works in the south.

The 38 letters: _____

Quote: _____.

5-61. MASTERING APOSTROPHES

Each sentence contains one mistake dealing with the apostrophe. Correct the mistake and write the correction on the line next to the question's number.

1. _____ He works in the mens' department in the clothing store.

2. _____ The coaches do not like his' yelling at the officials.

3. _____ Mr. Smiths' pen was mistakenly taken from the room.

4. _____ How many ts' are in that word?

5. _____ Wasn't the found purse her's?

6. _____ This certainly is someone's else's book.

7. _____ Why does'nt the conductor open the door in this hot train?

8. _____ Who'se job is it to close the gate?

9. _____ We happen to think that this is your's.

10. _____ Reggie wanted to open the buss'es windows.

11. _____ His sister's-in-law ring was polished by the aide.

12. _____ Bill's and Marian's car was sold to the new neighbors.

13. _____ This is nine dollar's worth of seafood.

14. _____ The game has already lost it's appeal.

15. _____ This will probably be found in the young adult's section.

16. _____ It was her's decision to drive to the tournament.

17. _____ Somebodys' license was found near the office today.

18. _____ The phone number was not their's.

19. _____ The awards were given posthumously to the ten hero'es wives.

20. _____ Our's is the last car in the last aisle of this lot.

5-62. DOUBLING THE NUMBER OF APOSTROPHE ERRORS

This activity tests your knowledge of apostrophes. There are four apostrophe errors in Paragraph A, four apostrophe errors in Paragraph B, and eight apostrophe errors in Paragraph C. Thus, the combined numbers of errors in Paragraphs A and B equal the number of errors in Paragraph C. Correct the 16 apostrophe errors.

Paragraph A. Last Wednesday we went to see my brother and sister-in-laws' baby, Connie. She is a real cute girl with big blue eye's and blond hair. Im happy that Connie is theirs' because I enjoy playing with little children.

Paragraph B. The tenth grade classe's reputation is of the highest quality. We have contributed generously to our school and our community. We have also built childrens' playground's, animal cages, and toys' for tots. The group members respect the rights of others and, as a result, get along very well.

Paragraph C. Bettys not had a moments rest since last nights' election victory. This morning she delivered a speech to the student's in the boy's gymnasium. The tenth, eleventh, and twelfth grade classes' attended. Then she spoke before the Women's Club and several other groups'. Tomorrow she will address the City Council member's.

5-63. THE MISSING 30

Thirty punctuation marks have been omitted in the following sentences. Insert them and be prepared to tell why you have done so.

1. When he calls for more information tell him that thirty eight people have signed up

2. Isnt this the correct sequence Helen

3. "My instincts are usually correct said the detective

4. Have you read Night by Elie Wiesel or To Kill a Mockingbird by Harper Lee

5. This document I believe is the answer to our prayers

6. Perrys wallet and Marcias handbag were left in the room after the assembly

7. Their car will be ready on Thursday they will pick it up around noon

8. Several residents went to the three local politicians offices however all the offices were closed

9. Shakespeares Macbeth and Romeo and Juliet will be performed this Thursday and Friday evenings

10. They should help you and I will see that they do so

Name _____ Date _____ Period _____

5-64. THE PUNCTUATION PUZZLE

Sixteen punctuation marks are the answers to this puzzle. One function of each punctuation mark is given as a clue, although some of these marks have several more uses besides the one given here. Review the marks of punctuation after you complete this puzzle. Write your answers in the correct boxes. Good luck!

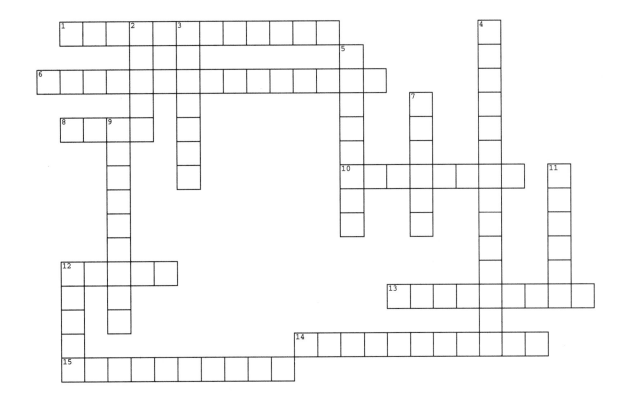

ACROSS

1. used after an interrogative sentence
6. used after a particularly forceful interjection
8. to indicate an abrupt change in thought, or a break in the sentence flow
10. three periods (suspension points)
12. used after the salutation of a business letter
13. can replace italics in certain situations
14. used to set off incidental information
15. to show the possessive case of nouns and certain pronouns

DOWN

2. used between lines of poetry quoted in running text
3. used to indicate titles of books, magazines, plays, and movies
4. used to enclose direct quotations
5. to enclose editorial corrections within a quoted passage
7. used after declarative sentences
9. used between independent clauses that are not joined by a coordinating conjunction
11. used to show where the word has been divided
12. used before coordinating conjunctions

5-65. WHY WE USE THE COMMA

Eleven of the 13 sentences in Group A are missing at least one comma. Insert the necessary commas within those sentences. Then, in the space next to each number, write the letter from Group B that explains why the comma(s) should be used in that particular sentence. Write the letters NN next to the two sentences that do not require any comma.

Group A

1. _____ After they left the mall the two cousins went to the movies.
2. _____ John there are more than one hundred meanings of that word.
3. _____ Finishing his lunch Ted was still talking about the World Cup matches.
4. _____ Perkins is a trusted valued employee.
5. _____ Our family visited the beautiful grotto located in Rome Italy.
6. _____ Moe Larry and Curly are The Three Stooges.
7. _____ The man was walking along the beach and he was listening to his Walkman.
8. _____ "There are new ways to increase your earnings" the clerk said.
9. _____ The new neighbors who are friendly are a bit too loud for my tastes.
10. _____ The problem is in my opinion very complicated.
11. _____ To help all those needy people Jim gave the best effort possible.
12. _____ She knew she could be happy wherever she went.
13. _____ We looked for the correct arrival gate and proceeded to head that way.

Group B

A. Use commas to separate an adjectival clause.
B. Use a comma after an introductory adverbial clause.
C. Use a comma to separate a city from its country.
D. Use commas to separate an interrupting expression from the rest of the sentence.
E. Use a comma to separate a direct quote from the rest of the sentence.
F. Use a comma to set off a name used in direct address.
G. Use a comma after an introductory participial phrase.
H. Use a comma to separate independent clauses.
I. Use a comma to separate items in a series.
J. Use a comma to separate consecutive adjectives.
K. Use a comma after an introductory infinitive phrase.

© 1999 by The Center for Applied Research in Education

5-66. THE REASONS FOR THE COMMA

On the line next to each sentence in Group A, write the Group B letter that explains why the comma is necessary. Use each Group B letter only once. Then, on the other side of this paper, write your own example sentence for each of the 12 reasons in Group B.

Group A

1. _____ John, you need to meet the new club officers.

2. _____ I want that piece of cake, but I also know it is very fattening.

3. _____ Since they chose to go to Miami, they have had offers from other cities.

4. _____ After the storm of last August, the residents spent much time cleaning up the debris.

5. _____ The beautiful, decorative designs inside that building are quite pleasant to one's senses.

6. _____ Gina's favorite athletic activities are soccer, gymnastics, aerobics, and jogging.

7. _____ The facts do show, in my opinion, the guilt of this accused man.

8. _____ "Take your best shot at it," Rich told his brother.

9. _____ Writing his memoirs, Henry learned much about himself.

10. _____ Dear Susan,

11. _____ Very truly yours,

12. _____ Jenny, who had researched her family's history, was moved by the experience.

Group B

A. Use commas to separate items in a series.

B. Use a comma after a direct address.

C. Use a comma after an introductory adverbial clause.

D. Use a comma to separate independent clauses.

E. Use a comma to separate a direct quote from the rest of the sentence.

F. Use a comma after an introductory participial phrase.

G. Use a comma to set off an adjectival clause that is not restrictive.

H. Use a comma after the closing of a letter.

I. Use a comma to set off an interrupting expression.

J. Use a comma between consecutive adjectives.

K. Use a comma after consecutive introductory prepositional phrases.

L. Use a comma after the salutation of a letter.

5-67. DETECTING THE COMMON WRITING ERRORS

The 13 groups of words in Group A contain common writing errors that are listed in Group B. In the space next to each number, match the example with the mistake and then write the letter that exemplifies that specific error. Each is used only once. The first one is done for you.

Group A

1. __C__ I can't ponder such a huge problem right now.

2. ____ Moving in the wrong direction, the marble statue was hit by the workman.

3. ____ "Are you willing to take responsibility for your actions" asked Martin.

4. ____ Each of the cathedral's bells have been checked several times.

5. ____ You could just as easily have done this your self.

6. ____ She said that she enjoys skiing a lot.

7. ____ The winner tried to console the looser.

8. ____ As long as they were given access to the county's files.

9. ____ When Sheila and Agnes met again, she told her what had happened last month.

10. ____ The interest group sought ways to motivate its constituents and the people respond in kind.

11. ____ Raised on a Kentucky, the legislator knew the value of hard work and determination.

12. ____ The problem is in my opinion much larger than we think.

13. ____ Fred knew the way to conserve his energy, and still run very strongly.

Group B

A. unclear pronoun reference

B. make this one word

C. avoid contractions in formal essay writing

D. unnecessary comma

E. use a more exact word or phrase to indicate a high degree

F. insert a question mark

G. insert commas to separate an interrupting expression from the rest of the sentence

H. insert the missing word

I. subject–verb agreement problem

J. verb tense problem

K. fragment

L. spelling error

M. dangling modifier

5-68. FINDING THE ELEVEN PROBLEMS

Eleven grammar, mechanical, and usage problems are found in these sentences. Each sentence contains one error. Match the error found in Group One with its description in Group Two by writing the letter on the line next to the appropriate sentence number.

Group One

1. _____ She acted in a prim and proper way.

2. _____ Last season our soccer team stunk.

3. _____ This form requires your signiture.

4. _____ I want to make you cognitive of the newly implemented procedure.

5. _____ The street's were lined with the New York Yankees' many fans.

6. _____ Her pastimes include stamp collecting, traveling, and to visit her grandchildren.

7. _____ "This will never happen again, he said to the workers.

8. _____ Ruining his plans for the upcoming vacation.

9. _____ How could this happen.

10. _____ Herman can't remember no facts about the case.

11. _____ Whenever a person complains, she will be heard by the right people.

Group Two

A. apostrophe

B. double negative

C. fragment

D. inappropriate usage level

E. incorrect mark of punctuation

F. misspelling

G. needless shift in number

H. parallel structure

I. quotation mark

J. trite expression

K. wrong word

5-69. WRITING ERRORS

The 12 groups of words in Group A contain errors in standard written English. In the space next to each number, write the letter from Group B that exemplifies the error.

Group A

1. ____ The author concluded that "Australia is unique is these ways"

2. ____ Two hundred protesters contained by the authorities.

3. ____ I read last night's assignment, Saki's The Open Window.

4. ____ He, unfortunately, is an obese, very heavy man.

5. ____ The cup was broken, its pieces were found in the dishwasher.

6. ____ "We will change trains tonight and be in Venice by mourning."

7. ____ This semester I will study harder be more organized go to extra help and concentrate better in my classes.

8. ____ Him and I did all the work by ourselves.

9. ____ While we was waiting in the dentist's waiting room, we talked about the upcoming vacation.

10. ____ We would of visited our grandmother every day.

11. ____ "It is getting too controversial for my tastes" remarked Paula.

12. ____ Wandering around for an hour, the building was finally spotted by the camper.

Group B

A. short story's title needs quotation marks

B. subject–verb agreement problem

C. end punctuation mark is missing

D. dangling participle

E. use commas within a series

F. insert a comma

G. redundancy

H. misspelling

I. fragment

J. comma splice

K. incorrect verb phrase form

L. pronoun problem

5-70. DON'T GET ANY OF THESE WRONG!

You know that in math, a negative times a negative equals a positive. In English usage as well, a negative and another negative equal a positive. Thus, in the sentence, "I **can't** get **no** satisfaction," the writer is really saying that he **can** get satisfaction since the two negative words—**can't** and **no**—make the situation positive or reversed.

Correct the double negative situation either by crossing out one of the negative words or replacing a negative word with a positive word such as, "I can't get **any** satisfaction." Write the replacement word above the word it is replacing. If there is no double negative problem, leave the sentence as it is. (*Clue:* There are nine sentences that have a double negative problem.)

1. I ain't got no friends.

2. You won't get nowhere unless you try harder.

3. This isn't no time to fool around; let's get serious.

4. Mickey didn't feel nothing after seeing the sad movie.

5. They will change nothing in the interim.

6. Their witness can't hardly remember what happened that night.

7. These drivers didn't try anything foolish during the exhibition.

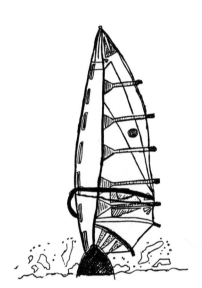

8. Henry has felt nothing different since he took the medicine.

9. My sailing instructor never told anybody about my little mishap.

10. They had not found none of the clues.

11. See if you can find a better television program, Meredith.

12. Nobody saw anything that looked suspicious.

13. You couldn't find no one to take your shift next Wednesday?

14. There isn't no way to get there.

15. We don't need no education.

5-71. A GLIMPSE AT THE COLLEGE SCENE

Some students applying to college take the SAT II in Writing. The questions in this activity are much like the questions they see on this examination. See how well you can do on these six questions. A portion of each section is underlined. The first choice simply repeats the underlined portion. The other three choices are reworded. Select the choice that most clearly and concisely expresses the intended thought.

1. Driving to school last Friday, <u>the accident was witnessed by Jason.</u>
   (a) the accident was witnessed by Jason.
   (b) Jason witnessed an accident.
   (c) the accident Jason witnessed.
   (d) Jason and the accident were spotted.

2. Both Jonathan Swift and Joseph Heller<u>, they had wrote satirical novels</u>.
   (a) , they had wrote satirical novels.
   (b) , they had written satirical novels.
   (c) they had written satirical novels.
   (d) wrote satirical novels.

3. <u>The Fourth of July, as well as Labor Day, are national holidays in the United States of America.</u>
   (a) The Fourth of July, as well as Labor Day, are national holidays in the United States of America.
   (b) The Fourth of July, and Labor Day, are national holidays in the United States of America.
   (c) The Fourth of July, as well as Labor Day, is a national holiday in the United States of America.
   (d) The Fourth of July, as well as Labor Day, is national holidays in the United States of America.

4. After the airplane landed at Heathrow, <u>we had waved to the pilot</u>.
   (a) we had waved to the pilot.
   (b) we, having waved to the pilot.
   (c) we waved to the pilot.
   (d) we have waved to the pilot.

5. Motion pictures, such as *One Flew Over the Cuckoo's Nest* and *Awakenings*, <u>helps to educate people concerning mental illness.</u>
   (a) helps to educate people concerning mental illness.
   (b) helps educate people about mental illness.
   (c) help to educate people about mental illness.
   (d) help to educate people concerning mental illness.

6. Mr. Bergen is one of those driven men <u>who wants to be the company's president.</u>
   (a) who wants to be the company's president.
   (b) who wants to be the companys president.
   (c) who want to be the company's president.
   (d) whom want to be the company's president.

5-72. IT IS NOW TIME TO ELIMINATE THE WORDINESS OF THESE GROUPS OF WORDS

This activity's title is a hint as to what you are asked to do on this page. Eliminate wordiness. Each sentence is much too wordy. On the appropriate line, write the clear and concise version of the wordy sentence. Use the reverse side, if necessary.

1. Mr. Hawkins stubbornly refused to bridge on the controversial issue.

   _____

2. In order that students who attend middle school can be successful, this program will be initiated during the month after September.

   _____

3. Jerry is going to be our club's next president by virtue of the fact that he accumulated more votes than the other people who ran against him.

   _____

4. The bus is running as scheduled at this point in time.

   _____

5. In the event that our car has a minor electrical malfunction, could you transport us to the place where the two pugilists will vie?

   _____

6. Her responsibilities include the replenishing of the sheets of paper for the copying machine, the typing of missives to people serviced by the law firm, and the answering of transported incoming telephonic signals.

   _____

7. It is quite important that in spite of the fact that it has precipitated in large amounts that domicile owners check the subterranean portion of their abodes.

   _____

8. The main function of the pedagogue of the English language is to furnish instruction for the young people in her charge.

   _____

9. We made a friendly waving of the arm and hand signal to the man who rents two rooms in our living quarters.

   _____

10. The novel entitled *Moby Dick* was written by a man named Herman Melville in the year 1851.

   _____

5-73. NOW *THAT* IS A MOUTHFUL!

The long, wordy sentence below needs immediate revision. On the lines below, revise this sentence into several more concise and effective sentences. You may add or delete words as you keep the original ideas.

Ever since I can remember, I have been a fan of the Dallas Cowboys football team, and I have sent away for their yearbooks and I also collect their trading cards which I never trade because I want to have every card of every player who ever played for this great football team, but I don't think I will ever have all the cards because some of the cards for the men who played over twenty years ago are not that easy to find, so I will have to be satisfied with whatever Dallas Cowboys' cards I can find.

_____

_____

_____

_____

_____

_____

_____

_____

_____

_____

_____

_____

_____

_____

5-74. UNLOADING SOME WORDS

Each sentence below is superfluous. Some words repeat what has already been said. Eliminate the superfluity by crossing out the extra word(s) in each sentence. Maintain the sentence's original idea. The first one is done for you.

1. The diver descended down to look for the treasure.

2. She was a seventy-year-old widowed woman.

3. Let us return back to the glory days.

4. What was the final outcome of the heated debate?

5. These are several of the necessary essentials.

6. Each and every one of the officials heard the blast.

7. He is a skinny, gaunt person.

8. I would like to greet my fellow classmates.

9. My older brother is more taller than you.

10. The deaf man who couldn't hear saw the closed-caption television program.

11. We are sure that the balloon will rise up again.

12. Will the argument recur again?

13. The unfortunate incident was clearly visible to my eye.

14. I do not want to repeat these words again.

15. Michael Jordan is the most unique basketball player.

5-75. TOO WORDY!

Each of these ten sentences is too wordy. On the lines, rewrite these sentences more concisely.

1. The committee will issue a statement regarding information that is of a confidential nature.

   _____

   _____

2. Our source is of the opinion the problem has a solution that can be reached in the immediate future.

   _____

   _____

3. Assembly members must give consideration to the fact that illegal aliens are crossing the country's borders.

   _____

   _____

4. All drivers who are currently driving on this road where this five-letter word's sign is placed must yield to the other drivers on the lanes next to them.

   _____

   _____

5. It is the decision of the town board that people who purchase a home and move into our town after tomorrow must obtain a card that identifies who they are.

   _____

   _____

6. The date that you propose for our Junior Prom comes into conflict with the date that has already been established for the school's Senior Prom.

   _____

   _____

7. Because of the fact that you were elected by the group as the new vice president, you must take an oath that swears to your allegiance.

   _____

   _____

8. The event that was the talk of the town was your winning the lottery.

   _____

9. Discontinue your progress and utilize your optical abilities.

   _____

10. Cease from creating oral communications.

   _____

© 1999 by The Center for Applied Research in Education

MOVING ON TO LONGER WRITINGS

5-76. GROWING PAINS

This paragraph could use some major improvements. It seems to be quite basic in its sentence structure and sentence patterns. Additionally, the paragraph suffers from errors in grammar, usage, and word choice. On the lines below, rewrite the paragraph by eliminating the errors and improving the sentences.

My dog is cute. Her name is fluffy. She is brown and two years old. We got her from Jodie who is my aunt. She works with a doctor. Who's name is Dr. Muller. Jodie is his nurse. Fluffy is a bagel with long ears. She is going to have puppies reel soon. My mom sez we can keep one pup and have to give the others to other persons. Who will like to have a little puppy. My sister and me maid a spot so where Fluffy can keep her little puppies. It is in the room where we keep our stuff for working on lawn and flours. We will play with our new puppy. And have fun.

_____

_____

_____

_____

_____

_____

_____

_____

_____

_____

_____

_____

5-77. AN EDITOR'S NIGHTMARE

Obviously, the person who wrote this paragraph was unhappy. Perhaps that accounts for all the errors. Then again, there might be many more reasons for the mistakes in this paragraph. Rewrite the paragraph correcting the errors you find. Even though a fragment is sometimes allowable in certain circumstances, correct this paragraph's several fragments and make them sentences. Compare your emended version with those of your classmates.

The activity in my neighburood has been annoying me this Summer. The children, who live behind me, is using there pool all most every day. They love to play a game called Marco Polo; drives me crazy!. All I here allday is, "Marco," followed by, 'Polo." This noice seams to make the dawgs bark moore. They can bark loud when thay chose too. Then the ice cream man. He plays that silley song, as he drives up the bloc. About three times a day. A nother disterbence is the konstant sawing fro the man nextdoor. He is building a poarch, he has been doing that for the passed two week ends. Lastley, the trucks who go up my streat are also noicy. The drivers speed, and do not care if it bothers people or even kids. Hopefully, my neighburhood will be coming quite once the skool year begins in Septemmber.

_____

_____

_____

_____

_____

_____

_____

_____

_____

_____

_____

5-78. TOO MANY I'S

One of the pitfalls of some writers is repetition. Variety is essential to effective writing. Unfortunately, this writer seems to be stuck in the "I" mode of starting sentences. On a separate piece of paper, rewrite the composition making it less redundant. Show variety in sentence starters by eliminating as many "I" words as you can. Share your rewrites with your classmates.

I was on a soccer team that was very good. I played sweeper for this team. I was coached by Mr. Benny Clark. I think that all the players on the team liked him.

I and my teammates had won the county championship and then headed for the state championships. I remember how we played Venny High School in the semifinal match. I saw Robin Trainor score the winning goal for our team and then we carried him off the field in our celebration.

I knew the state championship game against Cornwell would be a struggle for both teams. I could feel the tension before this important game and realized that all the players felt the same as I did. I heard our coach's last-minute instructions and heard our assistant coach tell the players to do their best.

I cannot tell you how exciting the game was that afternoon. I scored the opening goal and the Cornwell team answered back with two quick scores. I looked at the clock a little later and I saw that only two minutes remained. I and my teammates knew that we had to accomplish the nearly impossible task of scoring at least twice within the next one hundred twenty seconds. I felt my heart pumping faster as the seconds clicked away. I saw my friends, Paul and Harry, take shots that hit the post and careen away from the goal. I knew then that our team was destined to lose the state championship game that day. I also knew that we were not so good as Cornwell and that the better team won that game.

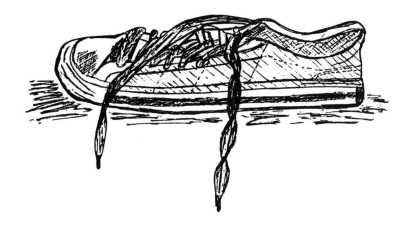

5-79. HERE'S TO THE EDITORS!

Your chance to see what an editor does each day is here. This paragraph has numerous errors. On the lines below the paragraph, rewrite the paragraph making the necessary corrections. It is not necessary to add words. Simply correct the existing paragraph. That is enough to do!

Each day this passed summer me and my friends went to the beach. Usually we would take the bus, or get a ride from a nieghbor. At the beach many familier people like to line their blankets and umbrellas near the water to get the full flavor off the sunny day. Some people like to lye on the blankts and read, while others enjoy walking along the beech. Young children usually play in the shallow water to build castles and dig tunnels. The lifeguards keep close watch on all the swimmers. Who go out to farr. Each of the lifeguards have been trained in CPR. So that they can save a victim's life. Only once have I saw a rescue, it was a successful one to! Hour days at the beech these last two months has been a memorable experience.

_____

_____

_____

_____

_____

_____

_____

_____

_____

_____

_____

_____

_____

5-80. OUCH!

Ouch! is an effective title for this activity. After all, to read something this poorly written truly hurts. There are 30 words that are spelled incorrectly. Circle these misspelled words. Then, above the misspelled word, write the word's correct spelling.

1. Though I am embarrassed, their are a couple of reasons why I don't wont to make a

2. seen. The principle reason is that what happened to me is not fare. I bearly did

3. anything wrong! When my car's breaks failed and I could not stop, I crashed strait

4. into too plastic garbage cans. A few of the people who live in that neighborhood

5. came out to sea what happened. It was quiet a mess! I herd what they said and

6. new that I had to show my patients in this case. I didn't no if I should pick up the

7. peaces of the cans or call the police. I could here a plain overhead and I remember

8. that a few drivers past bye and looked at the wreckage. Sum road by and

9. laughed; others looked very board. Fortunately, the homeowner who's cans I had

10. broken had the presents of mind to calm me down and tell me that I had to except

11. the fact that it was knot really my fault. She told me that if I paid for the cans within

12. three weaks, she would forget the hole thing. This was a lessen I would never forget!

5-81. ASSESSING A PARAGRAPH

Read the following paragraph concerning Muhammad Ali, one of the world's greatest boxers. Then, on the lines below the paragraph, answer the questions. Discuss your answers with your classmates.

Muhammad Ali is probably the greatest boxer of all times. With a body resembling a Greek statue, powerfully long arms, and amazingly quick legs that allowed him to float like a butterfly, Ali was certainly a force to be reckoned with in any boxing ring. Intelligent, humorous, and well-versed, Muhammad could turn the pre-match press conference or even the match itself, for that matter, into a forum all his own. He brought entertainment wherever he went, be it Zaire, Manila, or Madison Square Garden, the most famous arena in the world. The most skilled of all boxers, Ali was also famous for his civil rights activism and his protest against the Vietnam War. Recognized today as an international hero, Ali, according to some, has one of the most recognized faces in the world.

1. Is there a thesis statement? _____ If so, write it here.

_____

2. Is the thesis statement supported by specific details? _____

3. If your answer to number 2 is yes, cite several details. _____

_____

_____

_____

4. Are these examples presented in an interesting fashion? _____ If so, why? If not, why

not? _____

_____

_____

5. What suggestions would you have for improving this paragraph? _____

_____

_____

© 1999 by The Center for Applied Research in Education

Name _____ Date _____ Period _____

5-82. WHAT'S IN A PARAGRAPH?

Read the following paragraph and then answer the questions that follow. Write your responses on the appropriate lines. The sentences are numbered for your convenience.

(1) He was different. (2) Not just in the way he spoke, but in what he said, and what he did, and how he did it. (3) Tall and handsome, he commanded everyone's attention the very moment he walked into any room. (4) His clothes, sporting the look of the wealthy, were fashionably styled to match his mansion, his limousine, and his yacht. (5) People had spoken about his luxurious parties, his year-long vacations, his numerous servants and maids. (6) How had he come upon such wealth? (7) And why did he create such curiosity, such celebrity? (8) Yet, despite what others saw and thought about him, the defining moment of his life was yet to come. (9) It would happen when no one was near, when the city's bustle had ceased, when the children of the suburban commuters were fast asleep. (10) Yes, he would be talked about, but what would they think of what had become of him? (11) Only time would tell.

1. What is the paragraph's topic sentence? Write it here.

    _____

2. List three characteristics of the paragraph's character. For each one, offer a supportive example.

    _____

    _____

    _____

3. What is the purpose of sentences six and seven? _____

    _____

4. What is the purpose of the word *Yet* in the eighth sentence? _____

    _____

5. What is the purpose of the word *Yes* in the tenth sentence? _____

    _____

6. What mood is created by the pargraph's final sentence? _____

    _____

7. What is the purpose of the second sentence? _____

    _____

8. List two sentences that employ a series. _____

    _____

9. Why did the author use the series mentioned in the previous question? _____

    _____

10. Assign a title for this paragraph. _____

5-83. THE CD DILEMMA

You ordered five CD's from a company called CD SENSATIONS. You sent the company a check for $80.45, covering the cost of the CD's, shipping, and handling. Three weeks later, only three of the five CD's are in the box that arrives at your house. Needless to say, you want all five CD's. Since CD SENSATIONS offers no telephone customer service, you must correspond through the mail. Thus you must write a letter to resolve this situation.

On a separate piece of paper, using the information given below, write a business letter to CD SENSATIONS explaining your dilemma. Inform the president, Doris Baccio, how you would like the situation handled. Compose clear, direct sentences, and select effective and convincing words. Be firm, not nasty. That is not the way to handle this problem. Use today's date as the letter's date. Use your home address as the location to which CD SENSATIONS can send its letter. Use the space below to take notes or to write a scrap copy of your letter.

Company: CD SENSATIONS, 417 Altoona Blvd., Massapequa, NY 11758
Company President: Doris Baccio
Day that you ordered the CD's: five weeks ago today
Day that the box with only three CD's arrived: two days ago

5-84. A LETTER IN NEED OF REPAIR

The body of this resignation letter needs much better proofreading. On the lines below, correct the mistakes. Use the back of the sheet if you need more space. Remember, it is only the body of the letter.

Needless to say; these next few sentences are not that easy to write; I have worked for the Baldino Brothers Construction Company for the past twelve year's—and I have been very pleased with my treatment as an employee? The treatment afforded me by the owners and management have been second to nun. However; this passed January my family and I decided we would like to live in another part of the country. After visiting several states—we decided to build a new home in Main. Our precent home has all ready been solded and the builders are neerly finished w/our house outside of Bangor.

That being the case, I here bye tender my resignation effect a month from today. Please now that my years with the Baldino Brothers Construction Company has been most enjoyable. As we head up to Main? I want you to know I appreciate all that you have done for my family and I.

_____

_____

_____

_____

_____

_____

_____

_____

_____

_____

_____

_____

5-85. BECOMING MORE SOPHISTICATED

The following sentences tell about the life of the famous poet, Robert Frost. Though they are informative, they are not written with much maturity or sophistication. So here is your chance to present this information with more style. Assuredly, your reader will appreciate your effort to include more compound, complex, and compound–complex sentences. You might think about writing at least two paragraphs instead of one as presented here. Include as much of the given information as you can. Write your improved version of this information on a separate piece of paper.

Robert Frost is a poet. He was born in San Francisco, California, on March 26, 1874. In 1885 his father died and his family moved to Lawrence, Massachusetts. In 1895 Frost married Elinor White, his high school sweetheart. Frost studied at Dartmouth College for one year (1893–1894) and then studied at Harvard College for two years (1897–1899). Frost lived in England for three years. Frost published *A Boy's Will* and *North of Boston*. Both of these were collections of poems. In 1915 Frost moved to a farm in New Hampshire. In 1919 Frost moved to Vermont. In 1923 Frost had <u>Selected Poems</u> and <u>New Hampshire</u> published. <u>New Hampshire</u> won an award. This award is called the Pulitzer Prize. In 1938 the wife of Robert Frost died. In 1939–1942 Robert Frost taught at Harvard College. For the next six years, Frost taught at Dartmouth College. In 1942 Frost won an award for his collection of poems called <u>A Witness Tree</u>. This award was also a Pulitzer Prize. In 1961 Robert Frost read a poem at John Fitzgerald Kennedy's Presidential Inauguration. The title of the poem he read was "The Gift Outright." Two years after reading that poem Robert Frost died. The date of the death of Robert Frost was January 29, 1963. The place of Robert Frost's death was Boston. This is in Massachusetts. His gravesite is in Bennington, Vermont.

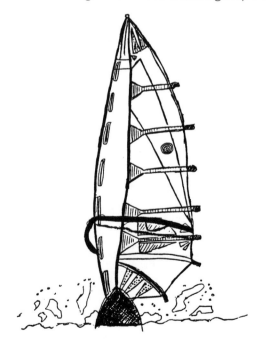

5-86. TRANSITIONS

Eleven transitions are listed below. Each is used only once. Write the transition in its proper place within the paragraph. To make it more of a challenge, each transition is written in lower case, though some of them will have to be capitalized to start the sentence.

and	but	in other words
also	first of all	in fact
another	for example	since
as it is now	if	

As a tenured professor at this college, I think that the current evaluation system certainly has its merits, (1)_____ I (2)_____ feel that it leaves room for improvement. (3)_____, the system needs closer supervision. (4)_____, the administrators should observe the professors at work. Come into our classrooms. To merely rely upon the hearsay of several students and other professors is ludicrous. (5)_____, how can one assess a tenured professor's teaching style and interaction with his or her students if that teacher was not observed in the classroom during the year? (6)_____, it would be much like a hospital administrator evaluating a surgeon's operating techniques without the administrator's stepping into the operating room to watch the surgeon at work. (7)_____ needed improvement is the inclusion of the professors and students in the evaluation process. (8)_____ professors are the ones in the classroom with their students, why not include both parties in the evaluation? (9)_____ only administrators formulate the survey's questions and criteria, (10)_____ students and teachers do not have a voice, I only see trouble ahead for everybody. (11)_____ we all may regret that we even had such an evaluation tool.

5-87. JOINING THEM

Below are twenty sentences that can be combined in a number of ways. Combine them into no more than eight sentences. Write your sentences on the lines at the bottom of this page.

1. My brother's name is Gary.

2. He is my twin.

3. I was born three minutes before Gary.

4. Gary likes to play baseball.

5. I like to play soccer.

6. I don't like baseball that much.

7. We usually get along.

8. Sometimes we argue over silly things.

9. Most of the times we argue it is about doing the chores that Mom and Dad tell us to do.

10. We have to clean our room.

11. We have to walk the dog.

12. We have to take out the garbage.

13. Gary and I take the bus to school together.

14. Our bus stops right in front of our house.

15. We sit together on the bus.

16. The bus is old.

17. Its number is 62.

18. Mr. John is our bus driver.

19. He is a friendly man.

20. My mother gave Mr. John a present in June.

_____

_____

_____

_____

_____

_____

_____

_____

5-88. PUNCTUATING THE DIALOGUE

Here is a dialogue between two young people. Punctuate it properly. If necessary, use your grammar book or another source to help you.

This is awkward Tony confessed I have never had a girl say something like that to me before

It should come as no surprise Karen remarked because you have been acting strangely for the past few weeks

Tony responded Why didnt you tell me earlier Then I could have tried to do something about it Now that you tell me I can sort of see what you mean Why did you not say something before this

There was never really an appropriate time I felt that if I said something to you your feelings would be hurt Maybe I should have told you this before today Im not really sure

Is there anything that I could do to try and make the situation between us work out I do think we can make it if we try

Tony you know what good times we have had Karen said I am not sure after all this that it can ever be the same between us Its not all your fault either I am also part of this problem

What do you think we should do asked Tony in a rather pleading voice Give it time

I need time to think about all of this Karen answered Its not an easy decision but I am willing to think more about it and then we can talk Okay

5-89. SUPPORTING THE THESIS STATEMENT

Good writers use strong supportive examples to defend their theses. Here you will do the same. For each of these eight thesis statements, write three supportive examples to support the topic sentence.

1. Surfing requires great patience and coordination.

   _____
   _____
   _____

2. Though running has its benefits, it also has its drawbacks.

   _____
   _____
   _____

3. Religion plays an important role in many cultures.

   _____
   _____
   _____

4. The Women's Liberation Movement has allowed women to be more successful in business and industry.

   _____
   _____
   _____

5. Today's teens live in a world quite different from the world their parents knew when they were teens.

   _____
   _____
   _____

6. The lyrics of today's rock music are very controversial.

   _____
   _____
   _____

7. Using animals for scientific experimentation is cruel.

   _____
   _____
   _____

8. The voting age should be lowered from eighteen to sixteen.

   _____
   _____
   _____

5-90. THE FINAL WORD: USE A BETTER WORD

Writers strive to use the best word to express themselves. This activity asks you to do much the same. Match the general words in Column A with their more specific forms in Column B by writing the three-letter answer on the blank next to the correct number. Then write the 20 three-letter answers (in order) on the line at the bottom of the page. If your answers are correct, you will have spelled out a quote by Alexander Chase.

Column A

1. ___ house
2. ___ writer
3. ___ road
4. ___ talk
5. ___ see
6. ___ steal
7. ___ waterway
8. ___ country
9. ___ aircraft
10. ___ liquid
11. ___ book
12. ___ furniture
13. ___ automobile
14. ___ instrument
15. ___ laugh
16. ___ walk
17. ___ run
18. ___ subject
19. ___ meal
20. ___ trait

Column B

(ADU) Italy
(CES) strut
(ENO) desk
(ESS) pilfer
(EWS) chat
(FUL) river
(ILD) breakfast
(LCH) social studies
(LTS) helicopter
(REA) essayist
(REF) boulevard
(REN) intelligence
(RST) guitar
(SFU) sprint
(SUC) guffaw
(TFI) sedan
(THE) mansion
(UCC) espy
(WER) thesaurus
(WHO) blood

Letters: _____

Alexander Chase's quote: _____

ANSWER KEYS

5-1. THE PLURAL PUZZLE

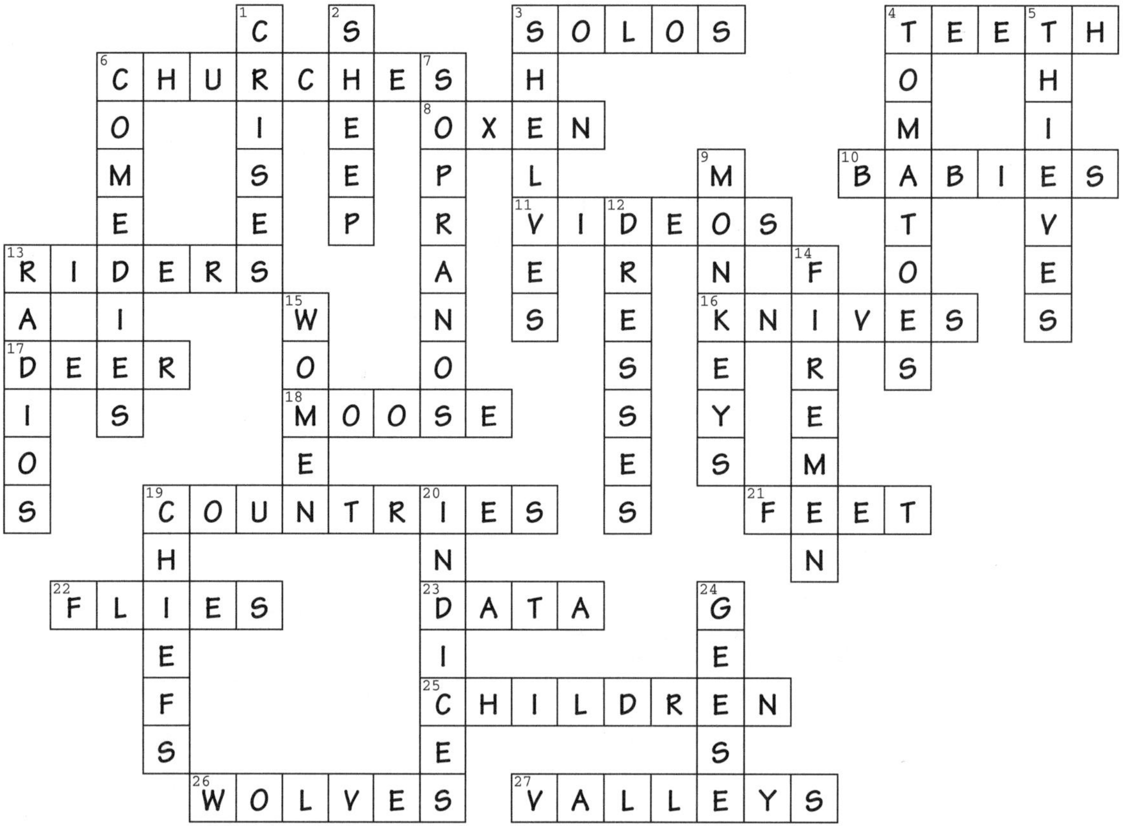
1 CRISES
2 SHEEP
3 SOLOS
3 SHELVES
4 TEETH
4 TOMATOES
5 THIEVES
6 CHURCHES
6 COMEDIES
7 SOPRANOS
8 OXEN
9 MONKEYS
10 BABIES
11 VIDEOS
12 DRESSES
13 RIDERS
13 RADIOS
14 FIREMEN
15 WOMEN
16 KNIVES
17 DEER
18 MOOSE
19 COUNTRIES
19 CHIEFS
20 INDICES
21 FEET
22 FLIES
23 DATA
24 GEESE
25 CHILDREN
26 WOLVES
27 VALLEYS

5-2. WORKING WITH PLURALS

1. rose
2. video
3. ox
4. datum
5. father-in-law
6. tomato
7. medium
8. deer
9. wish
10. mouse
11. louse
12. waltz
13. piano
14. woman
15. wolf
16. lady
17. child
18. thief
19. roof
20. knife
21. monkey
22. sky
23. fox
24. leaf
25. elf

5-3. THE ABBREVIATIONS PUZZLE

1. LIEUTENANT W A F
7. A H U I 8. B N O
9. REVEREND A 10. MEDICAL DOCTOR 11. ... R E T B O L U E E
12. ANNODOMINI D U N S M I E E A
E T 14. M O M A V R P
15. AND OTHERS N A I L
16. JUNIOR R 17. SENIOR 18. ... D E
U I T R N D I M
N 19. SOUTH AMERICA C E
E E 20. I L M
21. STREET U
22. COMPANY T D
T 23. VERSUS 24. MISTRESS
25. FLORIDA R N
R 26. HIGHWAY

5-4. WORKING WITH POSSESSIVES

1. June's bike
2. James's mother
3. Dallas's climate
4. laborers' wages
5. Romeo and Juliet's story
6. the union treasurer's speech
7. everybody's opinion
8. Poe's and Twain's stories
9. the Joneses' car
10. the media's attraction
11. their house
12. the cats' meowing
13. the three companies' plans
14. her hat
15. my father-in-law's wallet
16. the children's toys
17. the taxes' increase
18. the sixth day's activities
19. the author's family
20. Chris's eyeglasses

5-5. MRS. LIVINGSTON'S LIST

```
D H G T Z Q T M J N J Q X R Y Y S J Q D Q D C Y
V T J X G Q J F P F P N Q N S W N J Z G W C H V
C F L V X R V Y B T V B V J D X P C C K B Y V B
T O C M Q H F B K L Q J V V S M P Q C R F V Z N
Y Z U H M S L Z C K A R N S A D V J L J B P D D
N D L N Z L H P X S B P F G S L J L O N D L C L
V D E M C D J H P X Q A I V S T O T T M D A B V
T K R R M I Y W N T F B R C E T H O H E M I R N
F O R M A L L Y R L E S S E N Y K T S H O N E R
L A A Y L F H F P B W D M E T I P E E E W H A T
K L T T M N R M W A G N M M X E R H E F T K K W
X L L S H C K Q S D S I Z Q C T B P N Q C F V X
S U A Q R R J Y L M L T V C Y T H Y Q C D M K J
F D C N T Z E V Z P M W A H R C H Z C L S A Z M
C E L B B H D W M V N H K S I W Z E Q M E W M D
Y Q V F H Q L O C F L Z J H T F G B R W V X N G
M D W N N N C H J F S H W C Z M S T M E S F S F
```

5-6. WORKING YOUR WAY TO 45 WITH EVERY 2 OUT OF 5

The incorrect words and their correct forms are:

2. laid	9. right
3. moral	13. thorough
5. personnel	14. where
6. passed	15. while
8. quiet	

The total of the correct answers: 1 + 4 + 7 + 10 + 13 + 14 + 15 = 64.

5-7. WHEN IS A BUILDING RAISED?
WHEN IS A BUILDING RAZED?

```
S   B R A K E               D       P
T   R               Y       E       A
B A R E   K N O W     L E D   S I G H T
  T A   O   R A I S E   E L U D E     I
  I K   I       A   S   R   R         E
  O   C A P I T A L   D   S   T       N
  N   I   A   E       B E A R         C
  A   T   T   S     R   I       S I T E
R A Z E   I   E     R   T       T
Y     I   E   S     T             A
    C A P I T O L   E   B         T
    L   S   E       F O U R T H   I
    L       S           U         O
    U       S           E         N
    D       E           D
    E       N   B O A R D
```

5-8. THREE IN A ROW

1. I	6. C	11. C
2. I	7. I	12. C
3. I	8. I	13. I
4. C	9. I	14. I
5. C	10. C	15. I

Three I's are followed by three C's and so forth.

5-9. WORDS WE OFTEN CONFUSE

1. among
2. good
3. infer
4. past

5. sight

6. seam

7. altogether

8. flare

9. capacity

10. break

11. likely

12. imply

13. male

14. cannon

15. metal

A major concern for any homeowner is the <u>MORTGAGE PAYMENT</u>.

5-10. KNOWING THE DIFFERENCE

These are suggestions.

1. Pilfer is to steal petty objects or small sums. Rob is a more general term for taking something belonging to another.

2. Puny is even smaller than small.

3. Scrub means to wash with intensity.

4. Hilarious is even funnier than funny.

5. A mansion is a very large, luxurious house.

6. Guzzle is to drink greedily.

7. Terrify is to frighten greatly.

8. Stumble is to fall or miss one's step. Tumble is to fall clumsily or suddenly.

9. Save is to be economical. Hoard is to accumulate and store away.

10. Criticize is a general term for finding fault. Reprehend suggests strong or severe disapproval.

11. Uncooperative means not going along with what is suggested or directed. Belligerent implies taking actions that are likely to provoke a fight.

12. These two words are nearly synonymous. Charm is to attract or please greatly. Captivate is to fascinate.

13. Different is not quite the same as the typical. Grotesque is bizarre.

14. Mania is an intense degree of interest.

15. Jog is to run at a casual pace. Sprint is to run at top speed.

5-11. IS IT THE RIGHT WORD?

Group One's correct sentences that total 21 are 4, 7, and 10. Group Two's correct sentences that total 42 are 12, 14, and 16. Here are the corrections.

1. beside	11. dived
2. brake	13. from
3. borne	15. effect
5. burst	17. ensure
6. canvass	18. except
8. counsel	19. famous
9. medium	20. fewer

5-12. AVOIDING IDIOMS

1. annoying me
2. in a difficult situation
3. persevere
4. favorable position
5. confront a difficult situation
6. do two things at the same time
7. accusing one when another is just as guilty
8. overmatched
9. make peace
10. said the wrong thing
11. Pay attention.
12. cautious

5-13. CASTING AWAY THE CLICHÉ

Students should recognize that the clichés include *tried and true; gentle as a lamb; point with pride; cool, calm, and collected; easier said than done; beyond the shadow of a doubt; shouldered the burden; as wise as an owl; sneaking suspicion; sober as a judge; catching the kingpin; finding a needle in a haystack; hit the nail on the head; sadder but wiser; brought back to reality;* and *face the music.*

5-14. DON'T BE AS STUBBORN AS A MULE

1. irritating me
2. a difficult position

3. overcoming great odds

4. cope with it in a mature way

5. take on a difficult situation

6. make peace

7. totally

8. was overmatched

9. accomplish two things at the same time

10. one guilty party accusing another guilty party

11. injure one's own interests

12. favorable position

13. said the wrong thing

14. carefully

15. pay close attention to what is going on

5-15. WHAT EXACTLY IS ALL THIS?

1. gas station attendant
2. cemetery
3. desks
4. fire alarm
5. flashlight
6. lead pencils
7. toothpicks
8. hammer
9. robbery
10. bus driver
11. mud flaps
12. lies
13. firing

5-16. MAKING YOUR WRITING CLEARER

Answers will vary.

5-17. MRS. LINKER'S CLASS

1. exactly alike
2. calm and self-possessed
3. little hope of success
4. quite intelligent
5. very sturdy
6. very seldom
7. raining heavily
8. quite skinny
9. ancient; antiquated
10. dead
11. meek
12. quite warm
13. treat with care; treat tactfully
14. to eavesdrop
15. intelligent; very sharp
16. stop quickly
17. very sly
18. to be generous
19. to achieve success or fame
20. look everywhere

5-18. MRS. MALAPROP HAS TO GO!

1. hard place
2. sheep's
3. camaraderie
4. Inquisition
5. cognizant
6. salmonella
7. beautification
8. graduation
9. excise
10. alfresco
11. clenched
12. antidotes
13. innuendo
14. etiquette
15. harrowing
16. rabies
17. conformity
18. retention
19. akimbo
20. convenience

5-19. SEVEN-UP

1. F
2. F
3. RO
4. CS
5. CS
6. F
7. RO
8. RO
9. RO
10. F
11. F
12. CS
13. RO
14. CS
15. F
16. CS
17. F
18. RO
19. CS
20. RO
21. CS

5-20. SENTENCE OR FRAGMENT?

Fragments: 1, 2, 7, 8, 11, 12, 14; sentences: 3, 4, 5, 6, 9, 10, 13, 15

Quote: "Life is what happens when you are making other plans," John Lennon

5-21. OLDIES BUT GOODIES

1. S
2. F
3. F
4. S
5. S
6. S
7. F
8. S
9. S
10. S
11. F
12. S
13. S
14. S
15. S
16. S
17. F
18. F
19. S
20. S
21. S
22. S
23. S
24. F
25. F

5-22. COMPLETING THE INCOMPLETE

1. si (C)   6. fo (C)   11. an (C)
2. do (I)   7. ne (C)   12. da (C)
3. xo (C)   8. fa (I)   13. ha (C)
4. ze (I)   9. no (I)   14. er (I)
5. no (I)   10. th (I)   15. lf (C)

Expression: "six of one and a half dozen of another"

5-23. FIVE ACROSS

1. Fragment   6. Run-on   11. Fragment
2. Sentence   7. Run-on   12. Fragment
3. Run-on   8. Fragment   13. Run-on
4. Fragment   9. Run-on   14. Sentence
5. Sentence   10. Sentence   15. Sentence

5-24. A COMPUTER GLITCH (OR TWO OR THREE OR . . .)

1. The batter whacked the fast ball.
2. Place your books under your desk.
3. This is the best way to get to his cabin.
4. Our library is not open that late.
5. She is the school's best tennis player.
6. Two skunks were in our yard.
7. The family purchased a new motor home.
8. My favorite program is on tonight.
9. He just finished writing his economics term paper.
10. We waited for the comedian to arrive.
11. The room is in need of serious cleaning.

5-25. OUT OF ORDER

1. He will never go with that group.
2. Our band is fabulous.
3. The disk was found last night.
4. The darkened room is filled with strange objects.
5. I am asking you a question.

6. You should treat all people equally.
7. My parents want me to be a mathematician.
8. Gerald rolled the bowling ball down the alley.
9. He was sitting pretty.
10. All the points you make must be supported by facts.

5-26. STRINGING THE WORDS TOGETHER

Answers will vary. The following are examples.

1. After the storm subsided, the skies slowly cleared.
2. The police briskly stopped the group from wandering into the White House.
3. Suddenly two robbers emerged from the store.
4. The dented automobile that had crashed into the wall was moved into the garage.
5. We found a bracelet in the parking lot at the beach.
6. The doctor and nurse made an informal examination of the patient's toenail.
7. After the prom ended, the limousine was waiting by the restaurant's front door.
8. Yesterday Tom threw a cushion against the poster in his bedroom.
9. This morning the garbage man found our old cord and outlet in the street.
10. After the flood subsided, the weather brought some relief and we quickly forgot about the storm.
11. Both the trainer and the elephant were stunned by the gun's report at the circus.
12. While she was serving dinner in the mansion, the skeptical maid never looked more angered.
13. Our next door neighbor frequently takes his dog in the car with him.
14. Let the authorities know what happened to the victim.
15. Because we had to make an appointment, we took the ferry and arrived at the meeting within thirty minutes.

5-27. TEN OR FEWER

Answers will vary.

5-28. CONSTRUCTING SENTENCES BY THE NUMBERS

Answers will vary. The following are examples..

1. Stop.
2. Move it!
3. Hit the target.

4. The wall is painted.

5. Suzanne swam three miles yesterday.

6. The finest performers will be featured.

7. Two talented divers were paid to explore.

8. No magic wand could immediately solve these problems.

9. Grandfather's medication has helped him to rest more comfortably.

10. Can you believe that the Yankees are so far ahead?

11. While the adults played *Monopoly*, the younger guests watched television programs.

12. To improve their formats, most radio stations depend heavily upon listeners' recommendations.

13. If it rains tomorrow morning, the trip will be changed to another day.

14. Burned by the scorching sun, the lady who refused to wear sunscreen suffered terribly.

15. Whether you select this sweater or another one, I want to buy it for you.

5-29. LET'S EXPAND HERE

Answers will vary.

5-30. THEMATIC SENTENCES

Answers will vary.

5-31. HELPING MR. HOPKINS

Answers may vary slightly.

1. The weather was beautiful and we went swimming.

2. Since the mountain was breathtaking, we took a picture of it.

3. The American astronaut who walked on the moon in 1969 is Neil Armstrong.

4. Toni Morrison, the author of the novel *Song of Solomon*, is a famous writer raised in Ohio.

5. Bob Dylan and Jim Morrison were major forces in the music world during the 1960s.

6. When Luanne walked past the living room, she glanced at the people in there, but she did not speak to them.

7. Brittany, who won the race, heard the crowd cheer.

8. On Sunday the family went to church, walked to the park, and ate dinner together.

9. Since my sister had her baby yesterday, she and her husband are very happy.

10. Pleased by the witness's remarks, the detectives had some valuable leads in the case.

5-32. MATCHING THE SENTENCE'S TWO PARTS

1. A	5. L	9. D
2. J	6. C	10. I
3. F	7. G	11. H
4. B	8. K	12. E

5-33. QUOTATIONS

1. E	6. A
2. I	7. D
3. H	8. G
4. F	9. C
5. B	10. J

5-34. CRAZY QUOTATIONS

1. "Winning isn't everything, it's the only thing."
2. "The aim of education should be to teach children to think, not what to think."
3. "The only new thing in the world is the history you don't know."
4. "God helps them that help themselves."
5. "Power tends to corrupt, and absolute power corrupts absolutely."
6. "He serves his party best who serves his country best."
7. "Man is born free, and everywhere he is in chains."
8. "Those who cannot remember the past are condemned to repeat it."
9. "The most alarming of all man's assaults upon the environment is the contamination of air, earth, rivers, and sea..."
10. "If you don't say anything, you won't be called upon to repeat it."

5-35. THE BIG CONCERT

Numbers 4, 7, and 9 are acceptable; the others are not.

5-36. INDEFINITE PRONOUNS AND WATER

The correct sentences are: 2, 4, 6, 7, 9, 10, 12, 13, 14, 16, 17, 18, and 19. The letters spell the words *ISTHMUS* and *STRAIT*.

5-37. BE THE TEACHER

1. adverb
9. pronoun
15. adjective
18. verb
19. adjective
20. adverb

John Q. Public's score: 70%

5-38. FINDING A MATCH

1. C
2. R
3. A
4. D
5. L
6. E
7. T
8. O
9. Y

Two words are: CRADLE and TOY

5-39. PARTS-OF-SPEECH FILL-INS

Group One (15):
1. 2
2. 7
3. 5
4. 1

Group Three (15):
1. 6
2. 5
3. 2
4. 1
5. 1

Group Two (15):
1. 3
2. 7
3. 4
4. 1

Group Four (15):
1. 8
2. 5
3. 2

5-40. CLAUSES

Answers will vary.

5-41. DO YOU AGREE?

1. is (*not* are)
2. is (*not* are)
3. was (*not* were)
4. is (*not* are)
5. are (*not* is)
6. are (*not* is)
7. is (*not* are)
8. are (*not* is)
9. are (*not* is)
10. have (*not* has)
11. are (*not* is)
12. am (*not* are)
13. are (*not* is)
14. is (*not* are)
15. equals (*not* equal)

5-42. DETECTING THE WRONG VERBS

1. seen
2. sought
3. *correct*
4. rung
5. began
6. threw
7. frozen
8. shook
9. *correct*
10. swung
11. brought
12. rose
13. run
14. *correct*
15. shook
16. ridden
17. *correct*
18. burst
19. stolen
20. gone

Four names: MISS MARPLE, HERCULE POIROT, SHERLOCK HOLMES, and FATHER BROWN.

They are: detectives in literary works

5-43. HAS HE ATE THE WHOLE PIE?

1. ate
2. swum
3. grown
4. shook
5. hung
6. slid
7. fled
8. stung
9. rose
10. dreamed
11. ridden
12. raised
13. thrown
14. lay
15. written

5-44. USING THE CORRECT VERB TENSE

Verbs are used correctly in A, D, E, K, L, N, O, P. The two types of bodies of water are LAKE and POND.

5-45. IRREGULAR VERBS

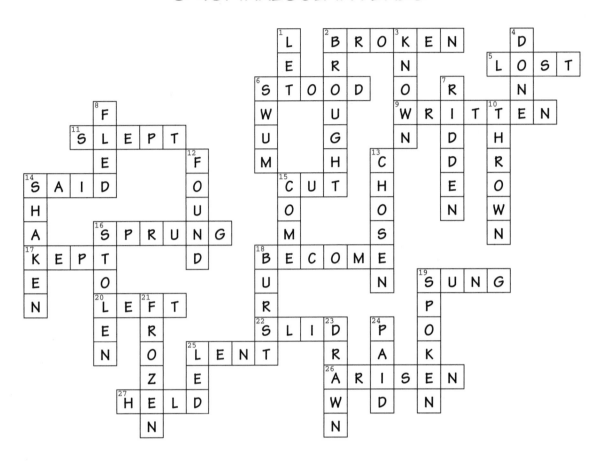

5-46. DOING THE EIGHTY-ONE

1. I; themselves
2. I; you
3. C
4. C
5. C
6. I; We
7. I; she
8. I; yourselves
9. I; us
10. I; its
11. I; she
12. I; their
13. C
14. C
15. I; He

$1 + 2 + 6 + 7 + 8 + 9 + 10 + 11 + 12 + 15 = 81$

5-47. DRIVING TO WORK LAST FRIDAY, DAD WAS IN BLOOM

Sentences 4, 7, 11, and 12 are correct. Here are possible answers for the other eight sentences.

1. While Roger skied down the hillside, the other mountain looked huge.
2. The doorbell rang after we washed the dishes.
3. The homeowner shot his gun while running after the intruders.
5. Weary from the strenuous workout, Hank placed the weights back in the closet.
6. The ballot should be filled out properly by the voters when electing a new president.
8. The teacher picked up the rubber ball thrown by the first grader.
9. While she was doing her homework, Laurie was scratched by her cat.
10. To understand the intricate workings of the machine, you must study the parts.

5-48. LUCKY THIRTEEN GRAMMAR MATCHING

1. BE
2. CA
3. US
4. EI
5. TI
6. ST
7. HE
8. RE
9. GE
10. OM
11. AL
12. LO
13. RY

"Because it is there." Geo(rge) Mallory

5-49. DIAGNOSTIC TEST OF USAGE

1. Change *number* to *amount*.
2. Change *good* to *well*.
3. Change *less* to *fewer*.
4. Change *of* to *have*.
5. Change *which* to *who* or *that*.
6. Change *no* to *any* or change *can't* to *can*.
7. Change *theirselves* to *themselves*.
8. Change *between* to *among*.
9. Change *accept* to *except*.
10. Change *Being that* to *Since* or *Because*.
11. Change *ain't* to *isn't*.
12. Change *everywheres* to *everywhere*.
13. Eliminate *hardly* or change *can't* to *can*.

14. Change *Leave* to *Let*.

15. Change *in* to *into*.

16. Eliminate *he*.

17. Change *respectively* to *respectfully*.

18. Change *then* to *than*.

19. Change *effect* to *affect*.

20. Change *allusions* to *illusions*.

5-50. ONE TO A SENTENCE

1. *have landed* instead of *of landed*

2. *fewer* instead of *less*

3. *should not* instead of *hadn't ought*

4. *doesn't* instead of *don't*

5. *Regardless* instead of *Irregardless*

6. *It's* instead of *Its*

7. *besides* instead of *beside*

8. *most* is unnecessary

9. *medium* instead of *media*

10. *off* instead of *off of*

11. *There* instead of *Their*

12. *most* is unnecessary

13. *who* instead of *which*

14. *at* is unnecessary

15. *healthy* instead of *healthier*

5-51. PROBLEMS . . . PROBLEMS . . . PROBLEMS

1. I	5. C	9. B
2. A	6. H	10. E
3. F	7. D	11. J
4. G	8. K	12. L

5-52. DO YOU KNOW YOUR GRAMMAR AND USAGE?

1. B	8. T	15. E
2. L	9. M	16. F
3. R	10. P	17. Q
4. C	11. K	18. G
5. O	12. I	19. D
6. N	13. S	20. U
7. A	14. J	21. H

5-53. ASSESSING SOME SKILLS

1. M	6. E	11. B
2. O	7. A	12. W
3. N	8. L	13. I
4. T	9. C	14. G
5. R	10. U	15. S

Words are: MONTREAL, CUB, and WIGS

5-54. NATIONALITIES ARE IN—TRUE OR FALSE?

TRUE: 2, 5, 9, 11, 12, 13, 14, 15; *spell out:* AMERICAN, JAPANESE
FALSE: 1, 3, 4, 6, 7, 8, 10, 16; *spell out:* CANADIAN, AUSTRIAN

5-55. TEN . . . TWENTY-SIX . . . SIXTY-FIVE

Group One (Total of 10)

2. Lilly and I (*not* me) . . .
3. Only we (*not* us) freshmen . . .
5. The winners are Kristine and she (*not* her).

Group Two (Total of 26)

7. Who (*not* Whom) told you that?
9. Please tell whomever (*not* whoever) you like.
10. Michael did it completely by himself (*not* hisself).

Group Three (Total of 65)

11. Both candidates, he and she (*not* him and her), . . .

12. The soda was drunk by him and her (*not* she).

13. It is I (*not* me).

14. Miguel is the one who (*not* whom) selected this restaurant.

15. The presentation was judged by Ms. Stevens and me (*not* I).

5-56. THE INFAMOUS TWENTY-FIVE

1. miniature
2. almost
3. necessary
4. unusually
5. suppress
6. chocolate
7. reference
8. inevitable
9. proceed
10. temperature
11. beginning
12. remembrance
13. acquired
14. influential
15. ninety
16. separate
17. teammates
18. occasion
19. recommend
20. mortgage
21. eligible
22. sophomore
23. sacrificed
24. aggravated
25. yacht

Three words associated with writing: manuscript, brainstorm, essay.

5-57. SPELLING SOLUTIONS

A crossword grid with the following answers: VILLAIN, INITIAL, EXERCISE, POTATO, TRAFFIC, RECEIPT, RECEIVE, REMEMBER, ACCURATE, SURPRISED, RECOGNIZE (among others).

5-58. COMPLETING THE SPELLING

1. auxiliary
2. announce
3. grammar
4. dominant
5. irrigate
6. remember
7. unprecedented
8. preferable
9. hoarse
10. controversy
11. cemetery
12. attendance
13. mortgage
14. noticeable
15. mathematics

5-59. SPELLING SUCCESS

1. S—amateur
2. P—twelfth
3. E—article
4. L—pursue
5. L—sacrifice
6. C—relevant
7. H—truly
8. E—remember
9. C—analysis
10. K—brief
11. E—vanilla
12. R—personally
13. S—appreciate
14. A—management
15. R—calendar
16. E—separate
17. N—heroic
18. O— cupfuls
19. T—dilemma
20. P—foreign
21. E—license
22. R—chimneys
23. F—patrol
24. E—wonderful
25. C—similar
26. T—temperature

Answers spell out: SPELL CHECKERS ARE NOT PERFECT

5-60. CAPITAL LETTERS

1. Wyatt, Earp, lawman
2. Europe, Africa
3. read, November
4. French
5. Republican, Orlando
6. Miss, Eccleston, Xerox
7. Prize
8. early, reformers, India's
9. Elizabeth
10. Northern, Canada, Express, Transit
11. Orioles
12. doctor's, office, ten
13. Halifax, east
14. regardless
15. Indigo, Girls, Harvey's, Tavern, Tampa
16. hilarious, interesting
17. niece, guy

"We learn from experience to do the right thing."

5-61. MASTERING APOSTROPHES

1. men's
2. his
3. Smith's
4. t's
5. hers
6. someone
7. doesn't
8. Whose
9. yours
10. bus's (or buses' or busses')
11. sister-in-law's
12. Bill and Marian's
13. dollars'
14. its
15. adults'
16. her
17. Somebody's
18. theirs
19. heroes'
20. Ours

5-62. DOUBLING THE NUMBER OF APOSTROPHE ERRORS

Paragraph A. Last Wednesday we went to see my brother and sister-in-law's baby, Connie. She is a real cute girl with big blue eyes and blond hair. I'm happy that Connie is theirs because I enjoy playing with little children.

Paragraph B. The tenth grade class's reputation is of the highest quality. We have contributed generously to our school and our community. We have also built children's playgrounds, animal cages, and toys for tots. The group members respect the rights of others and, as a result, get along very well.

Paragraph C. Betty's not had a moment's rest since last night's election victory. This morning she delivered a speech to the students in the boys' gymnasium. The tenth, eleventh, and twelfth grade classes attended. Then she spoke before the Women's Club and several other groups. Tomorrow she will address the City Council members.

5-63. THE MISSING 30

1. When he calls for more information, tell him that thirty-eight people have signed up.
2. Isn't this the correct sequence, Helen?
3. "My instincts are usually correct," said the detective.
4. Have you read *Night* by Elie Wiesel or *To Kill a Mockingbird* by Harper Lee?
5. This document, I believe, is the answer to our prayers.
6. Perry's wallet and Marcia's handbag were left in the room after the assembly.
7. Their car will be ready on Thursday; they will pick it up around noon.
8. Several residents went to the three local politicians' offices; however, all the offices were closed.
9. Shakespeare's *Macbeth* and *Romeo and Juliet* will be performed this Thursday and Friday evenings.
10. They should help you, and I will see that they do so.

5-64. THE PUNCTUATION PUZZLE

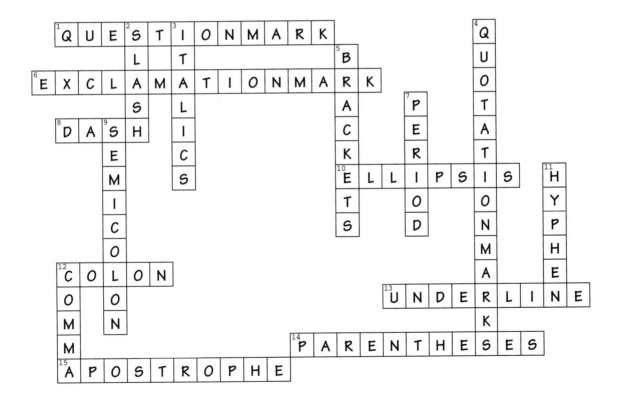

5-65. WHY WE USE THE COMMA

1. **(B)** After they left the mall, the two cousins went to the movies.
2. **(F)** John, there are more than one hundred meanings of that word.
3. **(G)** Finishing his lunch, Ted was still talking about the World Cup matches.
4. **(J)** Perkins is a trusted, valued employee.
5. **(C)** Our family visited the beautiful grotto located in Rome, Italy.
6. **(I)** Moe, Larry, and Curly are The Three Stooges.
7. **(H)** The man was walking along the beach, and he was listening to his Walkman.
8. **(E)** "There are new ways to increase your earnings," the clerk said.
9. **(A)** The new neighbors, who are friendly, are a bit too loud for my tastes.
10. **(D)** The problem is, in my opinion, very complicated.
11. **(K)** To help all those needy people, Jim gave the best effort possible.
12. **(NN)** She knew she could be happy wherever she went.
13. **(NN)** We looked for the correct arrival gate and proceeded to head that way.

5-66. THE REASONS FOR THE COMMA

1. B
2. D
3. C
4. K
5. J
6. A
7. I
8. E
9. F
10. L
11. H
12. G

5-67. DETECTING THE COMMON WRITING ERRORS

1. C
2. M
3. F
4. I
5. B
6. E
7. L
8. K
9. A
10. J
11. H
12. G
13. D

5-68. FINDING THE ELEVEN PROBLEMS

1. J	7. I
2. D	8. C
3. F	9. E
4. K	10. B
5. A	11. G
6. H	

5-69. WRITING ERRORS

1. C	5. J	9. B
2. I	6. H	10. K
3. A	7. E	11. F
4. G	8. L	12. D

5-70. DON'T GET ANY OF THESE WRONG!

The following sentences are possible answers.

1. I have no friends.
2. You won't get anywhere unless you try harder.
3. This is no time to fool around; let's get serious.
4. Mickey felt nothing after seeing the sad movie.
5. *correct*
6. Their witness can hardly remember what happened that night.
7. *correct*
8. *correct*
9. *correct*
10. They had not found any of the clues.
11. *correct*
12. *correct*
13. You couldn't find anyone to take your shift next Wednesday?
14. There is no way to get there.
15. We don't need any education.

5-71. A GLIMPSE AT THE COLLEGE SCENE

1. b   4. c
2. d   5. c
3. c   6. c

5-72. IT IS NOW TIME TO ELIMINATE THE WORDINESS OF THESE GROUPS OF WORDS

The following are suggested answers.

1. Mr. Hawkins refused to bridge on the controversial issue.
2. So middle school students can succeed, this program will be started in October.
3. Because Jerry won the election, he will be our club's next president.
4. The bus is on time.
5. If our car breaks down, could you drive us to the boxing match?
6. She fills the copying machine, types letters to the law firm's clients, and answers the phone.
7. Since it has rained heavily, homeowners should check their basements.
8. The English teacher's main duty is to teach her students.
9. We waved to our tenant.
10. Herman Melville wrote *Moby Dick* in 1851.

5-73. NOW THAT IS A MOUTHFUL!

Answers will vary.

5-74. UNLOADING SOME WORDS

Answers may vary. The following are suggestions.

1. remove *down*
2. change *widowed woman* to *widow*
3. remove *back*
4. remove *final*
5. remove *necessary*
6. remove *and every one*
7. remove *skinny,*
8. remove *fellow*
9. remove *more*

10. remove *who couldn't hear*
11. remove *up*
12. remove *again*
13. remove *to my eye*
14. remove *again*
15. change *the most unique* to *a unique*

5-75. TOO WORDY!!!

Answers may vary. The following are suggestions.

1. The committee will issue a confidential statement.
2. Our source feels an immediate solution can be reached.
3. Assembly members must consider that illegal aliens are crossing the borders.
4. Drivers on this road must yield.
5. The town board decided that new homeowners must obtain an identification card.
6. The proposed Junior Prom date conflicts with the established Senior Prom date.
7. Since you are the new vice president, you must take an oath of allegiance.
8. Your winning the lottery was the talk of the town.
9. Stop and look.
10. Stop talking.

5-76. GROWING PAINS

Answers will vary.

5-77. AN EDITOR'S NIGHTMARE

The activity in my neighborhood has been annoying me this summer. The children who live behind me are using their pool almost every day. They love to play a game called Marco Polo; this drives me crazy! All I hear all day is "Marco," followed by "Polo." This noise seems to make the dogs bark more. They can bark loudly when they choose to. The ice cream man is another problem. He plays that silly song as he drives up the block about three times a day. Another disturbance is the constant sawing from the man next door. He is building a porch and has been doing that for the past two weekends. Lastly, the trucks that go up my street are also noisy. The drivers speed and do not care if the speed bothers people, including kids. Hopefully, my neighborhood will be quiet once the school year begins in September.

5-78. TOO MANY I'S

Answers will vary.

5-79. HERE'S TO THE EDITORS!

Each day this past summer my friends and I went to the beach. Usually we would take the bus or get a ride from a neighbor. At the beach many familiar people like to line their blankets and umbrellas near the water to get the full flavor of the sunny day. Some people like to lie on the blankets and read, while others enjoy walking along the beach. Young children usually play in the shallow water to build castles and dig tunnels. The lifeguards keep close watch on all the swimmers who go out too far. Each of the lifeguards has been trained in CPR so that he or she can save a victim's life. Only once have I seen a rescue. It was a successful one, too! Our days at the beach these last two months have been a memorable experience.

5-80. OUCH!

1. there, want
2. scene, principal, fair, barely
3. brakes, straight
4. two
5. see, quite, heard
6. knew, patience, know
7. pieces, hear, plane
8. passed, by, Some, rode
9. bored, whose
10. presence, accept
11. not
12. weeks, whole, lesson

5-81. ASSESSING A PARAGRAPH

Answers will vary.

5-82. WHAT'S IN A PARAGRAPH?

These are possible answers.

1. The topic sentence is *He was different*.

2. The man was **wealthy** because he took year-long vacations, and he had fasionable clothes, a mansion, a yacht, a limousine, and servants. He was also **different** in the way he spoke and what he said and did. Lastly, he was **good looking** because he was tall and handsome.

3. These two sentences ask rhetorical questions for the readers to think about the character.

4. *Yet* introduces a transitional idea, the idea concerning the man's future and fate.

5. *Yes* emphasizes the fact that the man would be talked about and people would think about what had happened to him.

6. The final sentence adds some more mystery about the man and what will become of him.

7. The second sentence, really a fragment, explains how the man was different, the idea introduced in the paragraph's initial sentence.

8. Sentences that employ a series are sentence numbers 2, 4, 5, and 9.

9. Usually a series emphasizes a point by offering more examples as is the case in all four sentences listed in answer number eight.

10. Answers will vary.

5-83. THE CD DILEMMA

Answers will vary.

5-84. A LETTER IN NEED OF REPAIR

Needless to say, these next few sentences are not that easy to write. I have worked for the Baldino Brothers Construction Company for the past twelve years, and I have been very pleased with my treatment as an employee. The treatment afforded me by the owners and management has been second to none; however, this past January my family and I decided that we would like to live in another part of the country. After visiting several states, we decided to build a new home in Maine. Our present home has already been sold, and the builders are nearly finished with our house outside of Bangor.

That being the case, I hereby tender my resignation effective a month from today. Please know that my years with the Baldino Brothers Construction Company have been most enjoyable. As we head up to Maine, I want you to know I appreciate all that you have done for my family and me.

5-85. BECOMING MORE SOPHISTICATED

Answers will vary.

5-86. TRANSITIONS

The following is the original order. Students may want to argue for another order.

1. but
2. also
3. First of all
4. As it is now
5. For example
6. In other words

7. Another
8. Since
9. If
10. and
11. In fact

5-87. JOINING THEM

The following possible combinations.

I was born three minutes before my twin brother Gary.

Though Gary likes to play baseball, I don't like it that much since I like to play soccer.

Though we usually get along, we argue over silly things such as the chores Mom and Dad tell us to do.

My parents want us to clean our room, walk the dog, and take out the garbage.

Gary and I sit together on the old school bus, number 62, that stops right in front of our house.

My mother gave Mr. John, the friendly bus driver, a present in June.

5-88. PUNCTUATING THE DIALOGUE

"This is awkward," Tony confessed. "I have never had a girl say something like that to me before."

"It should come as no surprise," Karen remarked, "because you have been acting strangely for the past few weeks."

Tony responded, "Why didn't you tell me earlier? Then I could have tried to do something about it. Now that you tell me, I can sort of see what you mean. Why did you not say something before this?"

"There was never really an appropriate time. I felt that if I said something to you, your feelings would be hurt. Maybe I should have told you this before today. I'm not really sure."

"Is there anything that I could do to try and make the situation between us work out? I do think we can make it if we try."

"Tony, you know what good times we have had," Karen said. "I am not sure after all this that it can ever be the same between us. It's not all your fault either. I am also part of this problem."

"What do you think we should do?" asked Tony in a rather pleading voice. "Give it time?"

"I need time to think about all of this," Karen answered. "It's not an easy decision, but I am willing to think more about it and then we can talk. Okay?"

5-89. SUPPORTING THE THESIS STATEMENT

Answers will vary.

5-90. THE FINAL WORD: USE A BETTER WORD

1. THE
2. REA
3. REF
4. EWS
5. UCC
6. ESS
7. FUL
8. ADU
9. LTS
10. WHO
11. WER
12. ENO
13. TFI
14. RST
15. SUC
16. CES
17. SFU
18. LCH
19. ILD
20. REN

Alexander Chase's quote: "There are few successful adults who were not first successful children."